LOST SANDSTONES AND LONELY SKIES AND OTHER ESSAYS

By

Jesse Stuart

ARCHER EDITIONS PRESS

LOST SANDSTONES AND LONELY SKIES AND OTHER ESSAYS

Design by Wanda Hicks

Library of Congress Cataloging in Publication Data

Stuart, Jesse, 1907-
Lost sandstones and lonely skies, and other essays.

1. Nature--Addresses, essays, lectures. 2. Nature conservation--Addresses, essays, lectures. 3. Christmas--Addresses, essays, lectures. I. Title.
QH81.S875 081 79-18066
ISBN 0-89097-014-9

In my essays, I have tried to capture what is not so much in the news of yesterday and today and tomorrow. It doesn't take these subjects long, no matter how well written, to be hackyned, outdated and forgotten. But the fresh, rural approach that will always be with us. Wildlife, flora and fauna are immortal subjects. So is the subject of people. What is more interesting than people, just more of them. I've tried to write my essays on just place, not second place subjects. I want to give them to the readers to remind them of what is around them that they are overlooking. I want them to be pleasant reading, non-controversial. I want my readers to have something other than the media, which we receive each day, over and over again until it becomes boring and tiresome. I wouldn't write an essay about murder, rape and the big payoffs for all the money. I'm too sick and tired of these. I've had enough of these to do me the rest of my lifetime.

Maybe, I'm speaking here of "escape reading"—but I don't believe I am. I think I'm speaking of essays here that I have written that will have big appeal to the reading public who want to get away "from it all" and go into another, a quieter and saner world. I know we must meet and face pressures and try to solve them. But there should be a balance of pleasantries in our lives, in our thinking and reading. We should have a balance of the pleasant with the unpleasant and the sweet with the sour if we are to live balanced lives and keep our sanities. Our today's world is lacking this balance.

In writing essays as in other categories of creative writing, I have and will take my chances on choosing words, not objectionable in homes, schools, and to the great majority of the reading public. Choice words I've chosen to express my thoughts. Shocking words could change the readers' emphasis on these words, deterring their following thoughts I have tried to express. I prefer the readers emphasis on thoughts instead of ill-chosen stunning words to attract their attention.

I haven't written anything in my life to please the reader. I have written my way to please myself and by doing this, I hope and think I shall please the reader. My writing has to be done my way. I am the creator and master of what I write. My writing is part of me. It has to be me. This is the way I've done my essays, with a lot of happiness, good feeling, and fun. The essay has been, can be, a pleasant category of creativity.

Jesse Stuart

Contents

Home in W-Hollow in 1943

I LIVE IN THREE HOUSES

When people speak to us about the house we live in, I know they mean our house with its windows, doors, floors, fireplaces, and roof. It means the place where we spend all the time we can and where we eat and sleep. But every time someone reminds me of the house I live in, I think of three houses. I live in three houses.

Everyone on this earth lives in the house he or she takes with him or her. This is the human body which we are given at birth. Many of us are endowed, mentally and physically, with attractive physical houses, while others are not so fortunate. Many are compelled to live in weak bodyhouses, always in need of repair. And many do not live in the most attractive houses. But they constantly seek to improve their unattractive houses and make them more attractive. This is true among women. And why not? Why doesn't each woman and man constantly try to improve her house or his house from youth to old age—to make it a stronger house in youth so her body or his body can withstand the elements and time and have more endurance. This body each of us carries around is our most important house. This bodyhouse of ours is the one that builds the other two houses.

I was fortunate to inherit a strong bodyhouse. If I had not inherited a strong one, I doubt that I could or would have endured. I never had the balanced rations, and sometimes not enough rations, to give my bodyhouse fuel for heat, for mental and physical energies. But I was endowed with a bodyhouse that gave me great physical strength and endurance. There were very few young men (or middleaged and older as my bodyhouse moved upwards through the decades of years, ten, twenty, thirty, forty, fifty and now into beginning sixties) that could do more physical work than I.

In my youth I used my bodyhouse to physical extremes at manual and some mental labors. But in my young years and older ones, I never indulged in things that hurt or destroyed my bodyhouse. I never drank intoxicating drinks. I never put smoke into my mouth until I was twenty-eight—and then I didn't inhale pipe and cigar smoke into the lungs in my bodyhouse. I never clothed my bodyhouse with extravagant expensive clothing. I clothed it modestly to give it a fair appearance for the thousands who have seen it. A part of my bodyhouse, my mind, directed all these acts. A part of what I earned with physical and mental energies, created in my strong bodyhouse, went for the buying of necessities, Naomi, my wife, and our daughter, Jane, and I desired.

At the age of forty my bodyhouse had such physical strength as to stand and lift four-hundred pounds of dead weight from the ground up to load in a wheelbarrow. Then came the time when my mind told my bodyhouse there were not enough hours in the day for it to do the things it was requested to do. It was not by indulgences but by overuse that my strong bodyhouse collapsed in my forty-sixth year. It was not until that time that I realized its true value—that when this house was gone, I was gone. Overwork was almost the undoing of my strong bodyhouse. There were only three chances in one thousand that I could hold onto this house in which I lived—from which I couldn't be separated in life. But extensive repairs were made over a two-year period and my bodyhouse has had to be under constant repair ever since the collapse to avoid deterioration and final destruction.

Through my remaining forties, my fifties, and beginning sixties I have treated my bodyhouse like an old friend. Time alone and normal use can weaken a bodyhouse. In these years my mind, sometimes impulsive and with uncontrollable activities, has had to submit to the needs and cares of my bodyhouse. Impulsive and strong—too strong now for my bodyhouse, because it is active all hours when it is not in restive sleep—my mind is fully aware that when my bodyhouse (in which it lives and thrives) goes, it will go also. By protective measures, by preventive repairs before more damage can be done, I hope to keep my bodyhouse through my sixties, my seventies, and on and on as far as it will last me. I call it my first, last, and only real house. I will in no way that I know ever neglect my bodyhouse again.

Now my second house is where I lived as a boy. It is the house where we came to live after my marriage to Naomi Norris. Actually Naomi and I have treated this physical house, this house in the W-Hollow wind, better than we treated our bodyhouses. We have renovated this old house three times to give it beauty and to give us more space.

When Naomi and I married, I was raising sheep, farming, and writing stories and poems for which I received very small fees from magazines when and if they sold. When we were married, I had had four books published. They had received excellent reviews but had not sold well. When we were married, I went to a bank in another county and mortgaged my five hundred sheep to borrow four-hundred dollars to renovate the old farm house, which Naomi wanted for our home, so we could move into it.

At that time, four cows occupied two of the rooms. The other two downstairs rooms and the upstairs room were filled with hay and grain. Due to barn shortage on my father's farm, he was using this house for a barn. But when I married Naomi Norris, she had other ideas for she loved this house and W-Hollow with a passion and wanted us to make our home here. This pleased my parents and relatives.

We tore the old rooms away and completely rebuilt the two rooms where the cows were housed. We renovated the other rooms where he had grain and hay. Happily, we moved into our home where there was no bathroom and no electricity. Electricity was only dreamed of then. We had one open fireplace for heat in which we burned wood. In our cookstove we used wood. I chopped the wood for both stove and fireplace. And we used kerosene lamps. But this was our house in the wind—in W-Hollow that would grow in size and furnishings.

Shortly after we were married, I brought in a Delco System, wired this house, and we had electric lights and a radio which didn't have to be operated by batteries. Also Naomi used an electric iron. She had grown up in Greenup, Kentucky where she had been used to modern conveniences.

After World War II we returned to our home in W-Hollow. We got electricity and this was great! Now we could do things; our old pieces of furniture and books had accumulated until we didn't have space. We renovated again and we expanded. We added our first bathroom, a new living room, and made our old back porch into a new kitchen. And we added three new fireplaces for we were still heating our house with wood and coal. We had traps in two of our fireplaces so we could take ashes out from the outside to avoid ash dust settling over our rooms.

Naomi was an excellent housekeeper. She made our home beautiful. Everyone who came in bragged on arrangements of furniture, choices of wallpapers for the different rooms, how flowers were placed over our house, and even the arrangements of bookshelves through the house. We thought we had finished expanding and renovating what we already had.

But there came the time when we had our third expansion and renovation. We had to extend our house over the Shinglemill Hollow Stream. Now it extended from one hill almost to the other across Shinglemill Valley. We added a very large bedroom, which we occupy today, and another bathroom. We added two bookshelves to this room for our accumulated books. And we had furniture and antiques that we had already purchased traveling over America and over Europe, Near East, Middle East and Orient, ready to be placed here and there over our home.

We lowered the ceiling in our old bedroom, where there was an attic above it, where children played, enough to make room in the attic to give us two bedrooms upstairs. We made our house in the wind in W-Hollow according to Naomi's tastes. When she wanted the right old piece of furniture for the right spot, I got it if it could be found. She ran the house and I ran the farm. She helped me and I helped her. We wanted our house because our bodyhomes lived here. We didn't try to make it a museum or a showplace either. We wanted our furniture to be serviceable. We don't have an old chair that is dangerous for one to sit on for fear of falling. We have good, beautiful old things that fit our house. And we have decorative things of beauty over all this house. It is our home and we love it.

When two Greyhound bus loads of people, owners of fine old Kentucky homes, were touring East Kentucky, they requested thirty minutes stop at our home. They left here three hours behind schedule. "Why did you keep this home hidden?" one asked. The fact is we don't keep it hidden. Floors here are walked over equal to the floors in a school house. But we have made our home for us according to the physical house and the furnishings inside. Why would we ever want to make our home a "showplace"? We live here. And this is the way we like to live and the way we want it. Mrs. Simeon Willis, wife of the late Simeon Willis, former Governor of Kentucky, who is now Executive Director of the Kentucky Heritage Commission and who led the tour here, gave this impression of her visit:

"Jesse Stuart has made a better mousetrap, figuratively speaking, and the world is almost literally making a beaten path to his door. Aside from his novels, poems and short stories, his creations include one of the most charming spots in Kentucky, his own home. In what was intended to be a quiet and secluded hollow in the mountains, the place where Jesse and Naomi Stuart live sees a steady flow of visitors.

"Groups of students come, not only from Kentucky but from adjoining states as well. Tourists by the score hope for a glimpse of this beloved and honored man. Friends and neighbors bring their young people whose language Jesse Stuart speaks, and their visitors from afar must be shown the author and scholar who is their neighborhood's greatest asset. And, it must be added, he is one of the most lovable human beings living today, with a heart big enough to encompass the whole multitude of our people and every inch of land in the Kentucky he so dearly cherishes.

"It is against great odds that all this takes place at W-Hollow in Greenup County, because the only course by which tourists can reach this beautiful spot is a one-lane gravel road. In spite of this they make their way to his door, as did two large Greyhound buses, carrying members and friends of the Kentucky Heritage Commission to visit the Stuarts a few Sundays ago.

"Jesse and Naomi Stuart's house, 'built for living and not for show' as Jesse described it, has in spite of them become a showplace. Jesse's hobby is buying neglected acres and turning them into beautiful grassy plots, resembling an English park where deer and all manner of wild game roam unmolested; and where hillside growth, all native to the area, is pruned and trained as beautifully as the grassy plots which it borders and surrounds.

"Naomi Stuart's hobby is her house, where she has a great collection of priceless books; indeed, at first sight it looks as if the walls of the whole house are book walls. On further inspection one sees her fascinating collection of art objects from all over the world, brought back from their extensive travels; her beautiful handmade window curtains, trimmed with Belgian lace; rugs from different foreign countries and some woven by native Greenup Countians; furniture collected from both their families' past and some chosen with great taste in antique shops.

"'This is a house of books and ideas,' Jesse Stuart says, 'and wherever we go, we always return to it.' To members of the Kentucky Heritage Tour it was more than a house. It was a personality, a combination of two good and noble people: Jesse Stuart, the great writer and equally great philosopher and teacher, with his sublime faith in the rightness of the Universe, a quality always inherent in great and good men; and Naomi Stuart, listening, accepting, responding and holding herself with as much dignity and charm as any of the wives of our ambassadors or diplomats. This was an experience not only of the mind but of the heart of every person who was privileged to be there.

"So the world makes a beaten path to their door. The road is so narrow that, when an automobile containing a man, his wife and two children from a neighboring state, looking for the Stuart's home, met our large Greyhound bus, we saw every occupant of the automobile instantly make the sign of the cross. We were told that three school buses have to pass on that road every day, and this is nothing short of a miracle.

"However, if the rest of the people in Kentucky have the opportunity and privilege of seeing what the members of the Heritage Tour saw, and of being restored and refreshed both mentally and spiritually by the two wonderful Kentuckians who live at W-Hollow in Greenup County, undoubtedly there will be many people crossing themselves when they meet on Jesse Stuart's picturesque but narrow gravel road, and deeming it a pilgrimage well worth the risk."

Now this is the second house I live in. This is the house where so many come to see Naomi and me and more want to come than we can have. This is our home in W-Hollow, a beautiful valley for we have made it beautiful by work and careful planning. We have done it on less dollars than anyone would ever believe. We have made our dollars count. There has been little waste. This is where we went to housekeeping twenty-nine years ago, where our daughter grew up and played in this valley, where five generations of my people have lived and still live. This is where we will live until our bodyhouses are resigned to Plum Grove dust.

Now my third house is a house which no one sees. I can't show it to anyone. It is my own invisible house which is separated from Naomi's for she has one too. In this invisible house I am compelled to live alone.

I began to build this house in my youth. I remember very distinctly when I was a high school student in Greenup High School and when I was hungry for food, one of my classmates wanted me to share with him stealing a quarter from a high school girl's sweater pocket. I refused and let my hunger gnaw at my stomach. He took the quarter and bought candy and peanuts. His hunger was abated. But in this decision I added something to my invisible house in which I alone must live.

In this house I have stored up the finer things which are a part of me. In this house I have spirit, with power and dream! Who ever sees the spirit of man? Who ever sees or knows the inner dreams of man stored in his invisible house? And what about will power and second effort? Can you see them? And what about the old verities of truth, honor, and beauty—maybe trite words but they're lasting and will always come through inhibitions such as we have today in our modern society. Shouldn't everyone have these in his or her invisible house? I have them in mine.

My invisible house hasn't a door or window. It has no locks and keys. In this invisible house where I spend too little of my time, I have things stored which I have acquired and created by experience and decisions in my mind on which my heart served as judge. These two, heart and mind, have had much to do with my conscience, which no one, not even I have seen. But I know this is another invisible in my invisible house that helps to guide my mind which directs my bodyhouse in every act.

I have a supreme faith in the Creator of the Universe, who runs His universe with law and order. I am sure He knows about my invisible house, that He, invisible Himself has peeped into it—that He knows that I am His son for He knows my faith and beliefs are a part of this house.

My invisible house is full and bulging with invisible things. I have to have this house before I can operate my other houses. My invisible or third house is my house on top of the others. There will be more of this house left than of the other two when I am gone. The dream, stored in my invisible house, has a way of living on and on.

The only way you can detect or even surmise what I have stored in this richest of homes that I possess is by my actions, my words spoken and written, and by my deeds, while my bodyhouse is alive and active. It is from the storehouse in my invisible house that my mind is guided and I do deeds that I am told.

It is from this invisible house that I have received help by faith, will power, and extra effort when the going has been rough for me. And it is from here that conscience guides me to make decisions, often against the mass thinking around me. Consciousness and my thinking have almost been totally at war with mass thinking. It has caused me to divide people into only two groups, Constructionists and Destructionists. It has shown me where the mass thinking has put emphasis on the wrong things for our society and neglected the old verities, one of which is right and will prevail in the end. In my invisible house is also the switchboard to my brain, which controls my activities and creates my dreams.

My most important house is my invisible house, my top house, the house I live in and no one sees me in this house, or my going to and from it. There's no material in it. It is built mostly of intelligence, mind, heart, and soul. This is my greatest house.

WHEN HEART AND DEATH LIE DOWN TOGETHER IN A LONELY LAND

This morning I planned to climb to the Seaton Ridge where I could listen to the high winds rock the frozen timber in its winter sleep. I wanted to climb to this distant red horizon where the snow lay patched on this high enduring hill. Where the snow had melted in the valleys, the ground was covered with stiff, cat-whisker stems of frost.

I wore my heavy wool socks and my light durable shoes so I wouldn't have too much weight for walking. I wore the heavy trousers to my most expensive suit I used to wear in the northern states when I lectured. I wouldn't be needing this suit to wear again for lectures. Now, I was wearing these trousers to insulate my body against the wind that blew over the flatlands of Ohio to strike our northern Kentucky hills with terrific force. Then, I wore my red wool shirt under my autumn-colored sport coat. This sport coat was loose from my broad shoulders. It had large side pockets for my hands, corn for the birds, notebook, loose papers, and fountain pen. The elbows of this coat were worn threadbare, but I didn't mind this. I dressed for comfort here on my island.

For this would be the last year for me to be confined on my imaginary island. This was a most unusual island since it was completely surrounded by land. This island could be anywhere in America—in any climate and zone, east, west, north, or south—for a man who has had to take it easy because he had had a brush with death. But the magic thing about my island was the fact that it had increased as my health had.

At first, the borders of this island were definitely the walls of a single room in a house. This one room was my world and my island. In this world, as the tick of time started for the new year, I heard the winter songs of the birds as I watched them through my window eating at the feeding place. I heard them speaking in musical voices in the vines above my window at night. I heard the winds roar over and around the house and through the vines in the eaves. The sounds of the birds talking and the blowing of the lonely winter winds became music. My island was a small world filled with symphony and song.

I have lived on my imaginary island, but I have never been isolated despite the "No Visitors" sign. How could I live by myself as long as there were a few people, multitudes of animals, birds, flowers, and trees, and about anything that walked, crawled, flew, grew, and blossomed. I had to be part of everything. And everything became a part of me. The songs I heard were vast symphonies. I heard them in the wind, day and night, as I lay in bed.

I lay in bed with death in my island world when I took notes with my old orange-colored fountain pen I had carried from 1922–1926. I was walking five miles to and from high school then. I was going to the pine grove at night to write themes for my high school teacher. I was a youth then and I lived on this same island. But I didn't live here writing my youthful songs very long until I went beyond.

Then, after living in the amazing outside world for twenty-eight years, I had a brush with death. Again, I returned to this little island where I was born. At first, I didn't want to return to this island surrounded by land. I didn't want to live like this. But I had to live like this if I lived at all. Lonely days and nights when I slept with death, I heard these soothing songs on my island. They were not regional songs.

There is no such thing as a regional or local-color song. A song is a song or it isn't anything at all. It might be called a noise without a melody. But a song can come from any region, anywhere, in any season, at any time. A song is something universal. A song can come from a crippled heart when a man has learned more about life. A man who has lain down with death can always hear a song.

When the borders of my island expanded to the six rooms of this house, where I could look from windows at different hills, my songs increased. I heard more songs in my hours of loneliness when no visitors for me were allowed. Then another expansion came for me when I could walk outside into the yard. From the bleak hills flocks of winter birds flew in for me to feed day after day. They alighted in the barren branches of the dogwoods in our yard where they sang for me. Ground squirrels, gray squirrels, possums, and rabbits came into my yard where I fed them and the birds together. They didn't bother each other. Somehow they knew that I, who used to be their killer, wouldn't harm them now. How did they know? This was the theme of my new song.

I had been reborn into a new song! Life was different, for I had learned its great value. I knew a universal love, which couldn't be confined to an island, to one people, country, or place. The new love from my rebirth of life was borne on wings and it had to soar.

I walked slowly by the late winter streams which were white ribbons of ice in the weak winter sun. These mumbling waters under the ice would not hide their talents from me. They sang their loud lyrics for me to brighten my small, bleak world. Wild birds who watched over me for the first time alighted near and sang their special songs. I thought all the winds of the earth blew in my direction. The wind sang for me as never before because I had found a new life with new time on my hands to spend.

I walked by the quiet waters in the little streams when winter left and spring came. I watched the different species of trees put on their new shades of spring green. I watched winter, who wouldn't give up, return to kill the flowers and leaves. Winter's song was a cruel one of hate and despair. But April was here now. I measured the beauty of April by walking a mile.

I discovered a world that made me sing.

Because everywhere I found a song! I heard singing of clean young winds in dogwood and redbud blossoms. I heard bees mumbling their songs of busy hours around the bright hours, of the clock. Everywhere the friendly birds nested, laid eggs, hatched young, and sang to them and to me. Love was the theme of all singing. They flew over the clean waters in singing streams. And they sang to waters and waters sang back to them. The squirrels barked on the ground and among the hollow denning trees! Everywhere my world was in tune and singing!

What a world I had rediscovered! I had forgotten that so much existed here. Since the new love in my heart was universal, I had escaped the narrowness of thought. My songs took to wings that lifted them as high as I was high. My thoughts were like the spiders I had watched spin their own bright strands to ride on winds toward the sun. Where had they gone? Where had the days of yesterday gone? I would never know!

By summer I had increased the boundaries of my world to the extent of a five mile radius. I found animals and birds and streams and growing things were my friends and associates and part of my song. Because everywhere, now there was singing as never before. Everywhere I went I heard a song. Since there was love in my heart, I was not searching for songs but they were searching for me.

Then, autumn came with a new setting. This was like moving new furniture onto the stage for a new scene in my drama. I had learned that any life—sheltered, realistic, rich, poor, dramatic, or undramatic—was great drama. I had learned these things as the days of this year ticked off around the clock. Because in this autumn, my world expanded until it had a ten mile radius. I seldom traveled across the physical extent of this world. Every day, somewhere, someplace, I heard a song. I had to record these, for sometime, maybe, I wouldn't hear so many. And I might not be able physically to record them.

I had returned to the place where I had started. Winds had stripped the trees of leaves, leaving their dark cold iron traceries silhouetted against the low, dark, winter skies. And the moods of the winds changed from poetry to music very often. The little streams were covered with ice. They were white, crooked ribbons in the weak winter sunlight. And the birds had returned to the feed boxes. Possums had come back to the house to spend the winter under the floor and in the tiles. The rabbits were back and the squirrels were dropping in very often for loads of cracked corn at the feeders. Time had run a cycle. The hand of the year had gone around the clock. Now, the hand of day was high on the face of Nature's clock as I was climbing up my last lap to Seaton Ridge. My shoes were whetting sharply on the frozen ground and the snow. And the small trees that I touched were frozen stiff and filled with winter sleep.

This was the day next to the last for me to record in my journal. Now, I wanted to look my world over again. From this high ridge I could see, since the clouds were clearing and the winter sun was brighter, the width and length of my dark upheaveled land. I could see the dark waves of paralleled winter ridges which were a part of my land. Since I had lain down with death, my heart and death had been lonely prisoners on this dark land. I had been lost in everything.

For the first time since I had been lost, I had found my life. I heard singing everyplace. I went in the direction of the singing where I found songs. This world was crying with songs. I had learned something of value and truth after escaping death. I had learned now that so many things I used to think important were very unimportant. The things I used to think unimportant were most important. Once, I had been first. Now I had become last. I had found a new life by losing that portion which didn't have value. I had heard the new music of universal love, joy, peace, and brotherhood.

Since death had once been so near, I could quickly decide on the things of value. I made no pretenses nor apologies for allying myself with these things of value after I had slept with death.

Now I stood on the Seaton Ridge looking in all directions as far as I could see. This was the right place to come. I could measure my physical world from here. I could see my small imaginary island world where I had spent the year. I looked up into the skies at the clouds spread like vast white shrouds so close above me. I looked at the distant horizons in all directions and they were no longer red, but they were bright horizons now.

Now, I felt physically strong again. Someday, like the spider on his silken thread flying the wind, I would leave this world with my new visions. For the first time, my horizons were bright and far. I had to lose part of my life to find myself.

Snow on the pines near W-Hollow

THE COLORS WINTER WEARS

When people speak of winter's drabness and emptiness I think of the many colors I see. Nearly everyone thinks winter is either all white or all dark. But what is prettier than a white winter? What color in any season is more attractive than a clean white blanket of snow spread over the valleys and level spaces? Something really nice to see is snow-covered landscapes and white rolling cloudscapes with an in-between of leafless dark trees to contrast with the white below and above.

Snow and cloud are not the only white colors in winter. Frost, which is often called the "breath of God," is delightful to see under a cold blue morning sky. I have stood for minutes inhaling and exhaling just to see my white breath go out and thin to nothingness in seconds on this cold blue air. I have watched my cattle inhale and exhale on a winter field. Inhaling and exhaling among animals and men on winter mornings is nice to see. It is a white air that will not stay long. White air is absorbed faster than white gossamer threads spun by spiders and lifted toward the sun.

When the bright winter sun rises, the white frost rises too in the form of little clouds. This is a part of the winter world, a rapture of white colors that must be satisfying even to those who think of winter as being a drab, colorless season. It is an unforgettable scene to see thousands of these small white clouds rising simultaneously toward the sun over the winter earth.

Icicles hanging from the cliffs look like large white teeth in the dark mouths of gray monsters. Tall sycamores with white, green, and brown blotches of bark line the Sandy River banks. These "ghost trees" give one an eerie feeling when he sees them on moonlit winter nights or when he drives along the Sandy River Road and his car lights flash on them. White balls of milkweed furze are carried over winter's empty fields like miniature clouds by the strong winds.

Then, there is ice over the zigzagging streams in the dark valleys, over the ponds, small lakes, and rivers. Although this ice is never as white as new-fallen snow, here it is very white when contrasted to the dark, empty, barren land on either side. And when the sun shines, these crooked ribbons of ice that follow the streams are bright winding paths of light that make one squint his eyes when he tries to follow them. There is never a time when a man walks out in this winter land that he cannot see white. Even the barren branches of our silver maples, which grow wild here, are white iron-tracery against dark winter skies. Winter white is over the landscape and it is in the cloudscape. This winter white, which is far more than spring and summer's white blossoms and skies, adds a great beauty to our winter world.

The complaint I hear from most people is that winter takes all the green from the earth. They who complain should know that winter retains a great portion of green. For instance, in any winter land where there are firs, pines, and cedars, we get deep-dark and lighter greens. In this land there are pines on almost every hill. These green pinetops sway with the bright lyrical winter winds when the earth is fast asleep under a blanket of snow, while above us the cloudscapes, as white as snow, move the way the winds are blowing. One can now see earth-clouds of trembling green. No one can ever tell me winter is not filled with green. Our Sandy River in winter is a turbulent, restless, ribbon of green water.

There are also acres of wild green honeysuckle scattered over this land. The frosts come and stiffen the green honeysuckle leaves, and the icy winds tear at them. Snows and sleet cover them for weeks, but they still remained securely fastened to their little vines. They will remain bright and green under the weak winter suns. The greatest enemies of the wild honeysuckle's green leaves are not snow and ice but flocks of sheep and herds of cattle and deer that like to devour these patches of green in winter.

All one has to do is look up into dead trees to find the green mistletoe. This parasitic plant grows from the dead trees or dead branches of old oaks, apple trees, sweetgums, and blackgums. In this area, just before Christmas, mistletoe is shot down with guns. Our gathering mistletoe for Christmas goes back to the old druid customs: We follow their practice of kissing under the mistletoe. On the dead or dying tree where mistletoe flourishes, men are afraid to climb. Their shooting this green parasitic plant from the tree is becoming another winter custom here.

Another winter green that is gathered by hundreds of our country youths is the mountain tea which grows close against the rocky hilltops, the place where mountain tea survives the best. Youths in this winter land have found the mountain tea, chewed its green leaves and eaten its red berries. A few of its leaves actually turn red while it is alive and growing.

One of the rare green trees which people in this area have had for Christmas trees and decorations in the past is the holly bush. Holly would grow excessively here if it were left alone. Forty miles from here it still grows in abundance. Several people do a lucrative business selling the green holly bushes and wreaths filled with red berries to the stores and to people in the cities to be used for Christmas trees and decorations. The green holly trees, which grow very slowly, are being pushed deeper and deeper into the mountains each year.

One of our bright winter greens that will never disappear is the woodmoss. I can see a green carpet of moss covering the slope of the hill from my window as I write. This woodmoss is the greenest green of winter. It is a plush carpet into which one sinks to the ankles when he walks. Where the land is poor on the wooded hills there are green carpets of moss. Everywhere, in ravines and around rock cliffs, are patches of lively winter-green bracken, sword fern, lacefern and delicate maiden's hair fern. If one will only look for green, it is all over these winter hills. One cannot escape seeing it on this winter land unless he fails to use his eyes.

Here and there are tiny bits of red that add their decorative trimmings to all of winter's colors. There are red berries on the holly bushes. And there are small red berries on many of the dogwoods and on the mountain tea. But wherever one finds a patch of red sumacs, and they grow everywhere here—in ravines, on slopes, beside the roads—there are cones of ripe red berries which look redder still against a background of leafless trees, of brown and dark. The sumac berries are not well-liked by birds and squirrels, but they are held in reserve for a time when other foods are hard to find. Then these berries are eaten. They are only eaten when we have an unusually hard winter. But they remain upon their slick, leafless bushes like giant combs on the heads of tall roosters.

However, in a land where there is not much red in any season but autumn, this color is scarce in winter. This might be the reason the flocks of red birds stay over the winter long. They are very happy about their bright red feathers as they go splitting the winter winds with their strong wings. And we are very happy that these birds choose to remain. Also, in our search for red colors in winter, we often find red sandstones on our slopes that we have never noticed before.

We often see red skies on winter days. We have seen the entire sky a mass of floating red clouds which makes a wonderful contrast when the earth is sunless and dark below. One so seldom sees a red sky over a snow-covered earth. But winter sunsets on the short winter days, when the earth is covered with snow, are the finest of any season. There cannot be any complaint from anyone that winter is totally without this color. For the sun in its setting often drags red clouds over its trail as it goes down beyond these dark hills on winter evenings. We see red horizons more often in the early mornings and the late evenings.

One might not think blue would be a winter color. But where is there one who has never walked on a clear December day, looked up through the barren branches of the winter trees to see a cold, blue, winter sky with branches of trees silhouetted against it? Anyone who has will tell you that a cold winter sky is as blue as a robin's egg. Anyone who observes the winter day knows the skies are bluer in winter and have more depth than in any other season.

Often I have walked out to stand under the leafless persimmon grove where frozen persimmons were still clinging to the barren boughs. When I picked up a stone or a stick to throw to knock loose some persimmons, I looked up toward the blue cold December and January skies to see these leafless, crooked, ugly branches with fruit still clinging etched in the high blue of a winter sky. It thrilled me to think that the cold season, winter, could hold a delicious fruit up against the winter blue.

The blue morning skies are the same color of

deep holes of water in the streams when there isn't any ice. Deep water is as blue in cold, clear, clean winter as the high endless skies are blue. And the sawbriar berries are a deep blue like that of deep water and endless skies. The greenbriar berries are a light blue, almost the color of blue skies before they turn to gray. There is never a winter day when the sun shines that this world is not roofed with blue. There is never a night when the stars and moon are shining that the cold winter night skies are not a dark endless blue.

The scarcest of all colors in winter is yellow. One sees it sometimes in last year's leaves when the snow is off and the sun has dried the carpet of leaves which earth uses for a blanket to cover itself while it sleeps. Then, too, there is often a fodder blade which the wind has blown from a cornfield and lodged in a tree. The crabgrass on old fields of corn and wheat stubbles on fallow and empty fields are light yellow.

And I have seen rocks as yellow as ripe pumpkins in the winter sunlight upon these hills, Unfortunately, where erosion has cut down into the clay, there is yellow dirt. There is a winter yellow that is deplorable to see. Where one sees this, he thinks this part of the earth is worthless. And where the ground is too poor to grow its own covercrop of weeds, or where a forest fire has cleaned these covercrops, there are small yellow patches over the earth. Stand on one of these high hills and look down if you have any doubts! And if you have doubts about all of America, ride in a plane in winter and look down over the earth.

You will see that yellow is still a winter color where the earth is scarred.

Brightness is definitely a winter attribute. There is more brilliance in the millions of shining particles of frost when the moon is up before daylight than in dew drops on a spring or summer morning. And when the sun rises over the frost on a winter morning there are millions of frost particles glistening bright enough to hurt one's eyes. On moonless nights earth is illuminated by so many millions of bright stars that I have watched rabbits run and play in the light. Perhaps there are more stars in a winter sky than in a summer sky; I have always been able to see twice as many on a clear, frosty winter night. On cold, clear, moonless winter evenings the Milky Way becomes a bright shining island in the azure depths of blue.

We think of winter too often as a sunless season. We associate winter with dark, foreboding, lifeless lands without color and scenic beauty. It is almost impossible to associate brilliance with winter since murky, drab, and dark are the words so familiarly associated with this season. There is more brightness in winter than in any other season. Objects that are bright in all the seasons are brightest in winter.

There are bright trails of ice over the winding streams and rivers in the winter sunlight. When snow covers the land and the sun shines the earth is so bright our eyes must adjust themselves before we can look upon its brightness. Who has ever seen the earth around him in a prettier brightness than in winter when it is snow-covered beneath a full moon light? Or a lesser brightness when the snow is illuminated by the soft glow of millions of bright stars? Since we have all of this brightness how can winter be so drab, so forlorn and lonely? Winter-bright is one color I'll never be able to see as much as I'd like in my lifetime.

Brown is winter's most prolific color. Most of the winter earth is wrapped in a brown blanket of old leaves. Brown leaves still cling to white oaks that rustle and cry with the wind.

Broomsedge in the old fields, cornstalks, grain-stubble, and many wild grasses are brown-patched over the winter landscapes. Everywhere on empty fields, on bluffs, and under leafless groves of sleeping trees is brown, brown, brown. High hills are often crowned with brown sandstone cliffs silhouetted against a blue winter sky. Even the very earth when it lies exposed is a rich brown color.

Then, with so many lively colors in winter, where is all that drabness that makes people so hostile to this season? Where is all the dark? Hills look dark in winter. Well, winter has that trait too. The barren bodies of leafless black oaks are dark. Often the winter nights are brooding, long and dark, but the stars send shafts of light to splinter this drabness. Because of winter's varieties of colors, I walk and write more in winter than in any season of the year. I find winter so wholesome, so colorful, so great that I hate to see each winter pass! I have only so many of these delightful winters to live and when one comes I live it to the fullest. I am saddened by each one's passing. While winter is here I shall take my long walks, night and day, fill notebooks with thoughts and impressions, and record the brief descriptions of some of the colors it wears.

W Hollow in the spring with Jesse and Jane Stuart

IN MOMENTS OF REFLECTION

Before I was married, I never owned a car. I never bought a car until I was thirty-two years of age. That was the year of my life when Naomi and I were married. For the next three years she did the driving, for I couldn't drive. Then Jane was born. I learned to drive the car at the age of thirty-five.

Our car was not a luxury. Our car was a necessity. Cars had been advertised as something luxurious for almost a half century. And I don't have any intention of getting rid of my car. There are not any busses that pass our house. There is not a railroad or a streetcar line. We live in a valley walled-in by hills. Our car is our lifeline for getting out! It is something we can use in an emergency as well as for pleasure. But our car, and about everybody's which our present-day civilization has demanded of us, hurts us physically.

After I learned to drive I rode just about everyplace in comfort and I started getting soft. I stopped my walking. I had been a great walker. I didn't think about distances of twenty-five miles. I'd walk to the Riverton post office, a distance of approximately five miles. I had time to observe the wonders in the world around me. Each time I walked to the post office, I found something new.

I was younger then but my legs were as hard as dead seasoned locust. My leg muscles were powerful. I had developed these muscles by walking and climbing hills. My father and mother were great walkers, too, as they never owned a car in their lives. My three sisters could walk miles. My brother was a better walker than I, since he was taller. Since we didn't have a road leading to my father and mother's home, walking was the only way we could go from or return to our home. We carried loads home on our backs. My mother and father would walk to Greenup and carry two baskets of farm produce which they bartered for groceries. They were always physically fit. All of us, parents, sons, and daughters, stayed in good physical condition.

It had been four years since I had walked five miles to Greenup. Since automobiles are not infallible, something got wrong with my car, and it wouldn't start that morning. So we started walking, hoping we might get a ride. I had to take Jane to Greenup for an appointment. That was one beautiful summer morning. Flowers bloomed along the road. Jane had never seen them at all, since we usually passed them in our speeding car. Jane was so elated with so many wild flowers that we stopped and picked until she had a small armload and I had a large one.

Fortunately for us, no one came along to pick us up. We walked all the way to Greenup, where we gave our flowers to the girls who worked in the office. We gave three bundles to three secretaries, and they divided them with their friends. The walking that morning was a little tough, for it was much harder to walk on graveled and hard-surfaced roads than the old-time soft dirt roads. One's feet do not have enough spring walking on hard roads. Jane and I walked all the way to Greenup on graveled and hard-surfaced roads. But we enjoyed our walk. Our walk was a technicolored travelogue in reality. It was something to talk about. When we returned, Jane told her mother she wanted to walk to Greenup again.

Now, even if we and everybody around us want to walk to Greenup, we can't. We are no longer free to do these things. Someone would drive along and ask us to ride. The country has multiplied in population and almost every family owns a car. If a father doesn't own a car everybody feels sorry for him and is ready to pass the collection plate to get him a used jalopy. The slogan is: two cars for every family. Where will we put them, since there are larger and faster cars on the highways, that are a half century behind the progress of automobile making? Where will they go? Well, anyway, walking is obsolete. It is outmoded.

If everybody in a single community would take a notion to walk five miles to a little town and no longer use their automobiles, the press, radio, and TV would move in on the strange situation. Perhaps a few doctors and psychiatrists would come too. This would be a story of international importance. To have such great modern convenience and then to have a community rebel on using it! This just couldn't be real! This would make a better story than the man who whipped out his pistol and shot six times through his TV set.

Since we have ridden in our cars for so long, even if we have to go only two city blocks, we are expected to ride. Riding has become habit-forming. Riding has become a mental dope; a fixed, habitual part of our make-up; and a sickening state of helplessness that needs to be studied seriously by every normal parent and serious-minded youth in America. For a whole community of men, women, and children to start walking five miles and back would be an unusual thing. Ambulances would have to accompany them to pick up those who couldn't make this five-mile journey.

Automobiles are necessary things for Americans. The teenage boy in America works and saves to buy himself an old car. Automobiles have become almost as essential to our well-being as the bread we eat and the clothes we wear.

Highways have been built at great expense over this country, from coast to coast, across mountains, deserts, rivers, lakes, and quays. These were built for our millions of automobiles which have made walking so obsolete that muscles seldom ever grow hard in anybody's legs. Why should they? If it is true what scientists have said—that when a part of our human body no longer serves any purpose it disappears—then how many more centuries will legs and feet be a part of our bodies?

LOST SANDSTONES AND LONELY SKIES

From the Ridge Road I had seen the blue slate dumps where my father used to dig coal. When I saw them I knew not many days would pass until I would return. Now, with a stick in my hand, I walked up the path. I carried the stick for copperheads; this was copperhead country. Sweat ran down my face and dripped from my nose and chin. Sweat soaked my shirt-collar until it felt wet and limp around my neck. But I was happy to be on my way back to a desolate part of the community. I was happy my health permitted me to walk here. This was a forsaken section of sandstones, scrawny pines, persimmons, black sumacs, saw brier, greenbrier, pennyrile, and high lonely skies. The only vegetation that would grow here were the kinds that survived in a thin, starved soil. But fortunately for my father and my father's father, when they moved here there was coal under these sandstone hills to be mined.

I wanted to return to the place where I was born. I wanted to see once more the ugly mouths of the gaping mines in the slopes of these high desolate hills. Now I climbed up a path wagon-loads of coal had once rolled over. Cattle, mule, and horse teams had pulled the jolt wagons of coal, heaped high with big black lumps, over the winding indentation that was only a bare trace now. Once it was filled with tracks where animals had dug deep with their feet as they strained at their heavy loads. I followed this old road to the top of the ridge. Then I followed the ridge to a sand gap. Here I took the old wagon road to my right down the sandy point.

This old road had grown up in poison vine, bittersweet, bull grass, and briers. This was the first time since I could remember that this road had been overgrown. The ground had never had sufficient rain before to grow such heavy vegetation. But this season we had had plenty of rain. And through the years past, the dwarfed bushy-topped oaks growing along the banks of this ancient road had shed their leaves season after season, and these had rotted on the infertile land. These few old trees had done a splendid job of fertilizing the barren earth. Now the forest of worthless trees and briers was closing in. Soon this old road would be a part of the jungle.

I broke grapevines and bittersweet with my hands and pushed through this jungle growing in the middle of the old road. Often I had to lay my weight against the vegetation and push. Once I sat on the exposed roots of one of the old trees that had shaded the hot oxen many a time as they had toiled up this point with a load of coal from the mines below. This tree had shaded the mules and horses, too. Not many would think this bushy-topped oak had served a purpose in its earlier years. Well, it had. I could remember the long trains of mule and horse teams that left these mines with wagons of coal when I was a small boy. They went up this point, and they could go either right or left when they reached the ridge road. If they went right, they had to go over the hill by the Collins house and down W-Hollow to the E.K. Road and on to Greenup. If they went left, they had to go over and down the hill to the Womack Hollow Road, then to the Little Sandy River Road on to Greenup.

I walked down to the bushy-topped white oak. This tree stood in the yard of the house where I was born. But that one-room structure was in ashes now. In the spring of 1954 a forest fire, which burned over more than two thousand acres, got this little shack. This was my first time back to the scene since it had burned. And where this house had once stood, the ashes had helped to refertilize the ground and the weeds had grown taller. I could measure the exact spot where it had stood. Where the old garden was, someone had planted corn. This corn wasn't up to my shoulder. This was not land for corn. This was starvation land. It had always been. The Stuarts starved out when they moved here from Big Sandy. Everybody else had starved from this land. No one could have half-existed from the sustenance of this infertile land had he not mined the coal from under the sandstones.

Here I could smell the pennyrile, that aromatic herb which is death on insects, especially mosquitoes. But mosquitoes would never come to this hilltop where there isn't any water. There was a sulphur spring near the coal mine when my father and mother lived here. But this water was too full of minerals to use. My mother used to climb this mountain with a lard can of water on one hip and a child on the other. How my parents were ever able to live here, I never knew. And what was I doing here? Why had I returned?

The rabbit returns to the place where it nested in the ground. When dogs follow its tracks and hunters shoot, the rabbit returns to its place of nativity. This was the reason I was returning. I was born on this desolate spot of infertile earth, in a one-room shack without a doctor. In how many places upon this American earth, now desolate, forsaken, and forgotten, have America's children been born? America's ambitious children who have gone forward with starlight in their eyes, a dream in their hearts, and a prayer on their lips? Many of these have come from the inaccessible places, lost coves and hollows, beneath the high, spacious, lonely American skies.

No one passing could now tell that people had once lived here. The jungle had moved in. But people had once pushed the jungle back, mined the coal and raised gardens here among these sandstones beneath these high unfriendly skies. They had cut the sassafras, greenbrier, and saw brier with their garden hoes. They had salted the earth with their sweat to get only a meager pittance in return. Now they had mined out all the coal, and my people had helped. My people's sweat had salted the sterile earth of these sandstone hills. They moved away and other people came. They mined coal and worked the land for a bare existence. Now, all had moved away. All were gone. And the saw brier, greenbrier, wild grapevine, sassafras, persimmon, and scrubby pine were moving in.

I turned away from where the shack had once stood. I walked down the old wagon road toward the mines. The jungle had come over this too. But there were still prints of the road the way my father had walked. I found the place where scales used to be. Here was where they had weighed the coal when it left the mines.

From here, I broke vines with my hands and pushed my weight against the everlasting jungle. Finally I reached a high blue cone where vegetation didn't grow. Here was a clean place surrounded by bush, thorn, and vine. This was the old blue slate dump I had seen from a distance. My father had wheeled much of this slate from the coal mine above. Now the coal mine's mouth was a dark cavity, surrounded by earth's wooly jungle lips. The lips of this mouth were sealed tight. Vegetation would soon cover the mouth of this mine. I wondered how many times my father had gone back under the hill here. How many times had he lain on his side, on his back face up, and on his belly face down, and picked the coal from the seam in the days of long ago? How many times had he come from the coal bowels in this sandstone hill out into the sweltering heat of a summer day? How many times had he made a fire of coal outside the mine and sharpened his coal picks on an anvil? How many dreams he must have had here!

Now, this was a land where dreams were

buried. They were under this hill, in all directions the coal mine ran. They were every place under this hill where there was a mine entry. There were the old bank ties and wooden rails, turned dust or still preserved. Their dreams were deep deep down in this hollowed-out hill. Somewhere far away, men had burned this coal in the long ago. They, too, had sat before their blazing fires and dreamed. Giant teams had strained as the big wheels rocked under the heavy weight on the sandstone road. My father had seen the drivers leave the mine with loaded wagons for the scales. My mother had seen the teams pass on their way up the sandstone point to the ridge. And I, as a small boy, perhaps, had waved to the drivers when they passed. I never remembered these drivers. I might have met them as strangers in city streets in other towns in the later years of my life. And over this land I had walked with my father. He had held my hand in those years and led me to the scales and to the mine.

Now life once lived here, as in other parts of American earth, was a buried dream. Once it was a living dream that expanded, lived, breathed, and helped to build America! But now only the wind sighs lonesome songs, and the crows caw, and the sulphur stream of water flowing from a hole in the hill where the mine used to be mumbles sounds for those who once were here but who are now lost forever.

ARE WE A NATION OF DIGITS?

In World War II, when I served in the United States Naval Reserve, I was given a number to use instead of my name. I thought then that the number was merely a substitute for my name, that after the war ended I would get my name back. But have any of us? In the last twenty years the trend to substitute numbers for names has grown with such momentum that there seems to be no way to head it off. The number mania is like a large snowball rolling down a mountainside, sweeping its path clean.

I have already become a seven-digit telephone number. I'm 473-3813. "Is this No. 473-3813?" the operator asks. And I have to answer "yes" to get the call. My number used to be Grover 3-5613. I liked that, because it had a name on it. In those days I could call Sue, Nell or Tillie at the Greenup telephone exchange and ask them the time of day or what was news in Greenup. I'd call them by their first names and they would call me by my first name. Jesse sounds better to me than 473-3813. Jesse is a good old Hebrew name. I like it. But gone is Grover 3-5613, and gone is the Greenup telephone exchange. Gone too are Nell, Sue and Tillie. Gone is Jesse Stuart, for he is now 473-3813.

I've got more number names too. I got a gasoline credit card once, before driving to

California. My credit card was a number, ten digits, something like this: 132-577-5482. This was too big a number for me to tote around, even in my billfold. In disgust I threw it from my car window, onto the salt plains of Utah.

Now I've been told that I must have a bank number very soon and I won't be able to throw that away. Meanwhile, I sometimes get letters addressed to Occupant, Box 1000, Greenup, Kentucky, as if I had no other name. This makes my blood pressure rise. Some letters are merely addressed to Box 1000. To bring my blood pressure back to normal, I throw all these letters into the wastebasket without opening them.

I have never wanted to be called a number in my life. Not from the time I was a small boy at Plum Grove Rural School, when the teacher called our numbers in the order we had been chosen to come up front and spell. I resented being called a number then as much as I do now.

In our school there were forty to fifty pupils. Being Number One on either team was important to the pupil, perhaps more important to him than his name. Those chosen Number Two, Three, Four, Five and Six, among the twenty or twenty-five on either side, felt important too. But getting down toward the end of the line, I'd have a number such as seventeen or eighteen, if I were lucky, or it might be twenty-three or twenty-four. My number depended on how many took part in the spelling match—how many were in school, for everybody took part. If there were forty or fifty in school, they were divided into two groups, making the last pupil on each side Number Twenty or Twenty-five.

At Plum Grove, studying grammar like a hungry chicken foraging for worms in the springtime, I learned that a number was defined as a numerical adjective (adjective: kind, comparison, and use). I couldn't see a picture when I thought of a number. I could see only vague nothingness, a pale abstraction, a ghost rising from one of the thousand Plum Grove graves behind our little one-room school. I could see emptiness, space, an indescribable color of the wind. I hated the vagueness of abstractions. An abstraction was a mark which meant little to me. This was why I resented being called a number when I went up to spell. It was not because my number, nineteen or twenty-four or twenty-five meant I was such a poor speller that the team captain didn't choose me until the last.

When Carrie Burkhart, a pretty, blond-haired, blue-eyed girl who lived on a farm near Cedar Riffles, had her name called—which was always Number One—I wondered why the teacher did this. Number One was an abstract numerical adjective. Carrie Burkhart was a name to me—a person I had seen so often walking along a Plum Grove path in spring and summer, barefooted, with a blue ribbon in her hair. Carrie was a beautiful noun (noun: kind, number, gender, case and relations), a proper one, for it was the name of an important person, place or thing. When it applied to Carrie Burkhart it was a very beautiful and proper noun.

Then there were Clara Sinnett, Rhetta and Pauline Jordan, Edith Green, Martha and Minnie Howard, my cousins Grace, Essie and Eva Hilton, and my sisters Sophia, Mary and Glenna—all given these abstract numbers. I could not understand why nice names had to take numbers for substitutes—names so pretty in the mind's eye. When these names were called, my mind formed pictures. And there was music in the sounds of these names—music that reminded me of the wind in spring in willow leaves and in the frosted multicolored leaves on white oaks and red oaks in October.

Then there were the names of the boys: Everett Preston Hilton, Glen Hilton, Frank and Fred Hilton, my cousins; and Charlie Dials, Lonesome and Roy Perkins; Big Aaron Howard, Estil and Ramey and Little Edd Howard—all hunters and fishermen who went to school during the weekdays and hunted and fished at night. They loved hunting when they heard the wind in the pine tops at night and when moonbeams were coming through the pine boughs. These were my classmates, friends, neighbors, and playmates, and their names were stamped indelibly on my memory.

Just hearing the real name spoken let me see the image of one of my friends shaking a possum from a persimmon tree, or standing by a fire built on a high ridge and listening to our hounds chase a fox, or pulling a catfish from the Little Sandy River in the spring fishing season, which we always knew because red worms came to the top of the ground and crawled at night. Red worms made crazy hieroglyphics in the sand.

Then, my own name: I never thought it was as pretty when written on paper, blackboard or slate as some others. It didn't have the musical sound of many, but it was my name, and a name meant something more to me than beauty and sound and what our ancestors had done. The name belonged to me. I had to wear it, like my skin.

Sitting dreamily in the Plum Grove School, I thought my name would become a very respectable and pretty name if I did good things. If I did evil things, it would become distasteful, no matter how musical its sound or how pretty it looked written down. My name would be what I made it. Whether I made it good or distasteful, it would still be a proper noun and a picture image. And good or bad, my name would be more than an abstract number could ever be.

Later, when I played high-school football, I had a number on my jersey. But why not my name? I wondered. Later I was on a college track team, where I wore another number. I had to accept the abstract numerical adjective over the mental image and the music of the noun.

In later years, when I became a teacher, I put names to everything. I loved any and all names of my students over numbers. Each name meant something to me—an image, a musical sound, all depending on what my youthful student was about to pack into that name.

Names always mean more than numbers. I

remember the last year I was principal at McKell High School, South Shore, Kentucky, when Coach Ben Webb got so tired of numbers on his football team he decided to do something about them. Each player was a number and each signal was a number. Our quarterbacks and players had trouble remembering all the signals. We had mix-ups and confusion. We lost games. Then this brilliant coach stumbled onto an idea that caused him to win games and almost made him immortal. He changed signal numbers to the names of high-school girls his players dated. There were no more passes to the wrong man down the field and there was no more trying to go through the wrong side of the line. Our team began to win games and influence fans.

Each play, whether it was Betty Mercer, Nadia Ratcliff, Yvonne Bentley, Sabrina Tolliver, Janice Quillen, Marilyn Timberlake, Loretta Phillips, Sue Ellen Major, Carol Sherman, or one of a dozen other names, was executed without error. We won games and Ben Webb gained a reputation. Comments were heard up and down the sidelines at every game that our coach had the best set of working signals they had ever seen in football.

In this period of my life I thought I was through forever having to substitute numbers for names. I was wrong, though. When I joined the United States Naval Reserve in World War II, I had number 958-63-00 on my dogtag, which I kept on a little chain around my neck, and on a bracelet on my arm and on a piece of paper in my pocketbook, so that if I were killed at sea or on land they could identify my body.

After the war I said I'd never have another number, that I wouldn't be a numerical abstraction any more. Here is where I was fooled again. Because I didn't work for anybody, being self-employed, I didn't need a Social Security number—at least I thought I didn't.

Then, a few years after World War II, an attorney filling in my income tax return warned me I would now have to pay into Social Security, although I had been exempt as one who earned money not from wages. He said he had already obtained a number for me. He warned me I could not escape. So my Social Security number is 405-44-5654. It is too long, too abstract, too colorless to remember. And I haven't tried very hard to memorize it.

While I served in World War II, I did try to memorize my serial number, because there was hardly a day when I didn't have to give my number—not my name—to somebody. This somebody, another number, recorded my number on paper, making copies in duplicate or triplicate. Since I was an officer, I was expected to have enough sense to remember my number, instead of having to read it from my identification bracelet. But I never did succeed in memorizing it, and after the war I stopped trying.

Fourteen years later Kentucky voted a bonus for Kentuckians who had served in the Spanish-American War, World War I, World War II, and the Korean conflict. I had voted against this bonus, but I figured that because my taxes had to help pay for it, I ought to collect. I had to have my discharge to apply. I searched everywhere for this document but couldn't find it. I wrote to the Navy, asking for a photostatic copy, signing my full name, Jesse Hilton Stuart, to the letter. I thought my full name would suffice.

I waited a long time but received no reply. Then I wrote a senator from my state, asking if he could help me get my World War II discharge. In his reply he told me he had to have my serial number before he could do anything. I had forgotten my number. I searched everywhere for it. My wife, luckily, found my identification bracelet in her jewelry box. I sent this number to our senator in a hurry, for it was my number, not my name, that counted.

Recently, just before flying to the University of Florida to give a lecture, I received a letter from the member of the university's English Department who had invited me, telling me to be sure to bring my Social Security number, for I could not be paid without it. This brought up another problem. I had once carried my Social Security card in my billfold, but my billfold had been stolen with everything in it (including seventy-eight dollars) in Cairo, Egypt. And I couldn't remember the number at all.

So I drove off to the airport without my number, hoping that my name could substitute for it so I would be paid for my lecture. I was running low on money. It sounded crazy to me that I had to have my Social Security number before I could be paid. I thought, no wonder so many Americans have need of a psychiatrist.

(Luckily I found the number later on some old income-tax returns. I sent it to the University of Florida and they paid me.)

Maybe I'd made a mistake by not memorizing my Social Security number, or by not wearing it on a tag around my neck or having it engraved on an identification bracelet to wear on my wrist at all times. I had learned that digits—which might be called a collective numerical adjective—were what counted, instead of the name Jesse (Hilton) Stuart. Yes, I carried my name among neighbors and friends, and it was attached to stories, poems and articles in magazines and in literature textbooks; but owing to changes in America, this, my real name, was mere window dressing. My name, the one that had real meaning in Social Security and death, had been recorded for all eternity in groups of figures with dashes separating them. We are becoming, if we haven't already made it, a country where number substitutes have become names, and names have been reduced to substitutes. I wonder whether in years to come numbers will be more appropriate for tombstones than names. I suppose that for the sake of our descendants we had better have numbers marking our graves, so they can identify us without mistake.

W Hollow

NEEDED . . . A NATIONAL CLEANUP DAY!

We who live in W-Hollow have always tried to keep our meadows and pasture fields clean and our fences mended. Just about everybody who lives in this scenic valley has taken pride in keeping the premises clean. But will other people let us? No. If you came to W-Hollow today, and drove over the winding graveled road, on either side you would see all kinds of litter thrown from passing cars—soft drink bottles and cans, whiskey bottles, beer bottles (tin and glass), and even beer cartons. In several areas along our small, winding, beautiful road, people have even tried to create garbage dumps.

Seeing this debris along our roads makes us furious. Why wouldn't it make anyone furious? In our area each family tries to keep his small or large farm clean. Each sows grass on his meadows and pasture lands and he keeps forest fires from his woodland which brings, each spring, multitudes of wild flowers to match the dogwood, redbud, wild plum and wild crabapple tree blossoms. On my farm, where I have small creek-bottom meadows on either side of the W-Hollow Road, we have to take a crew to pick up the beer, whiskey, and soft drink bottles that have been tossed there from passing cars. From four to six times a year, we take a volunteer crew along our road picking up all the bottles and refuse strewn along our three miles of highway. I usually drive my truck and take two helpers. It takes us from a half to a full day to clean up our highway. Each time we clean up the road we get a truck-bed full of waste material. And our road is merely a connecting link between two state highways.

Before we cut our meadow grasses, we have to make sure all glass bottles are picked up from the meadows. We have learned to do this from a past sad experience. We had three large white-faced cattle waste away and finally die from eating broken glass in hay baled from our meadows. Now we practically take a fine-tooth comb in late spring just before cutting time when the grass is high and it is most difficult to see the bottles. Where the W-Hollow stream runs close to the highway, bottles are also tossed into the stream. We get these out of the water when we see them for many children like to take off their shoes, just like I used to do when I was a boy, and wade into the water in this stream.

Now, if you really want to see something, drive over our state and federal highways. I believe our highways in the New England States are kept cleaner than in any other part of the United States. On the other hand, anything can and does happen to highways in California. But for litter of highways, and pollution of small streams and rivers, not any state, unless it be Alaska or Hawaii, can be "not guilty." However, of all the southern states, or borderline states, Kentucky, one of the most beautiful states in the

Union, might take first place for litter along our highways and first place in stream pollution. Our closest rival, a state aptly named because of its scenic beauty, "The Switzerland of America," is West Virginia which might one day surpass Kentucky in highway litter and stream pollution.

If this is ever published, and if it finds a reader, I invite that reader to drive over the highways and byways of West Virginia and Kentucky and make up his own mind as to who deserves their First Place Shameful Honor. It grieves me deeply to think that our Commonwealth of Kentucky, with the first rated park system of all the fifty states in our Union, must have the most littered highways and filth-choked big and little streams and rivers in the United States.

When I leave the W-Hollow road, driving down State Route One to Greenup, which is only a distance of two miles, it makes me sick at heart to see bottles and cans so close in the ditch on either side of the highway, one can step on the cans and never put his foot on the ground. Down in front of houses that front on the highway is Town Branch, a stream between this row of houses and the highway. Litter is often thrown, not by all, but enough people to litter a stream that practically flows under their front porches. Down where the W-Hollow stream flows through the big culvert under the old Eastern Kentucky Railway and junctions with Town Branch, if you want to see litter drive along where the stream runs parallel to the highway. Here are many homes. I have seen people carry their litter across the highway and throw it into Town Branch.

In June either side of Town Branch is bordered with tiger lilies that bloom profusely, waving their golden blooms to passerby along this highway. Here could be a roadside stream of beauty. Instead it is one of filth and desecration. From here, one-half mile down the stream before the stream leaves the highway, there are at least 100 old tires thrown into the stream. There are bottles, cans, bushes cut and thrown into the stream instead of being burned; in front of one very fine home there is an old washing machine, half embedded in the bank of the stream around the front yard. If I could catch the people away from their nice home and if I could lift it, I would steal that old washing machine and take it to the dump in my truck. I am so tired of looking at this disturbing object.

One other area in our county which has a higher percentage rate than average for filth and strewn litter, is the Coal Branch Road. I mention this for a reason. Years ago this area was a German settlement. They didn't have the best land but they grew enough on this sterile soil to corner the vegetable markets in several nearby towns. They were good gardeners and farmers and many lived in modest homes but they were clean homes with well-kept yards. Today drive along this road. See the litter thrown behind these houses into the Coal Branch stream. These are third generation, maybe some fourth generation descendants living here from the old Germans and others who came down the Ohio River by boat and settled here more than a century ago. Even the mouth of this Coal Branch stream was used for a public dump which was close to Coal Branch Road and U.S. 23. This dump became so disgraceful the State Highway Department protested and stopped dumping here.

It is a pity some of these people, with their good German names, couldn't return to Germany, their ancient homeland, to observe the cleanliness of their ancestors. If they could go to Germany they wouldn't find a can along a highway. They wouldn't find any litter along their beautiful well-kept highways. The German people would never stand for this. What has happened to these old world people's descendants?

If you want to see something, if you think Germany is clean and beautiful, go to England. See if you can find litter strewn along the British highways. Go to Scotland, Wales, Ulster and Ireland. Note the cleanliness of the highways along their picturesque countryside. These above-mentioned countries furnished the lion's share of our early immigrants. What has happened to us since our ancestors had this sense and pride of cleanliness and beauty. Clean landscapes are also commonplace in Holland, Belgium, France, Switzerland, Denmark, Norway, Finland, Sweden, Hungary, Italy, Greece. And you won't find cans and litter strewn along a highway in Egypt, Syria, Jordan, or Lebanon. I know because

I've been there.

Many of our tourists overseas will stand up and tell the world boastfully how many more bathrooms our country has over any country in the world, how many more automobiles, how many more miles of good highways, refrigerators, telephones, radios, and television sets we have. All their statistics, I'm sure, are true. But one thing they don't dare boast about in the European countries or in the countries of the Near East and in parts of the Orient, particularly Japan, is the cleanliness of our highways. As my Uncle Jesse Hilton, for whom I was named, used to say: "Jesse, we are a dirty people." He'd been a great drinker himself but he never threw bottles and cans along a highway. And when he rode along and saw ditches on either side of the road filled with excessive drinking debris, he felt ashamed for us as a people. And he'd never been out of the United States. He'd never seen the clean highways of other countries, but he had a sense of what was right and proper and he abhorred the wanton destructiveness in our spreading litter along highways that had cost millions and billions of dollars to build.

Since the responsibility of keeping America clean in community, rural area, town, city, county, state, and nation does not fall on a few persons or a small group, it has to be everybody's job.

For a start, I propose that each State set aside a "Cleanup Day." Set this date sometime in May while spring is here and the landscapes are beautiful with grass, leaves and blooming flowers. This should be the month for "Cleanup Day." Make this day an annual affair, under supervision of teachers, school administrators and coaches to work with and supervise work of the students. Have the State Department of Highways (and I believe this department will cooperate beautifully) to take this day to help with cleanup. It will be imperative to use every truck they have to haul litter and refuse strewn along highways. Make this day a friendly get-together, a social get-together, all cooperating to do a job—to clean Greenup County (my county) which will help to clean our Commonwealth of Kentucky! If all other 119 counties cooperate, we'll really clean our Commonwealth. And if we clean Kentucky, forty-nine other states can do the same. We could make this a massive cleanup and beautification day. And look what a finer place it will make our community, our commonwealth, and nation to live.

Photo by G. Sam Piatt

W-Hollow

CONSTRUCTIONISTS VERSUS DESTRUCTIONISTS

Old Op came up the road in a hurry. He was dressed in a suit of heavy red woolens someone had sent him from Michigan. His weak eyes faced the cold blustery wind which still swept down this valley from the north. I watched him from my window. Naomi had gone to take Jane to school and I was here alone. When he came up the walk, I thought something had happened. Old Op was walking faster than his usual gait. I went to the front door and opened it.

"Come in, Op," I invited.

"No, I don't have time," he said. "I just come around to tell you that Enic Borders, the game warden, got old Jim Wythe."

"Jim Wythe's my friend," I said. "What did he do?"

"Your friend, my good eye," Old Op said emphatically. "The trouble is a man never knows his friend from his enemy. His enemy pretends to be his friend so he can do him dirt and get by with it. Jim Wythe, your good friend, tore down your state signs up and down the highway and let the strange hunters pour in all over your game preserve. That's all your good friend Jim Wythe has done!"

"You mean Jim Wythe did that?" I said. "It's hard to believe!"

"Yep, he drove this car out and stripped all the signs from the trees," Old Op said. "You know I have told you several times I didn't trust him."

"Did he go on this place and hunt?" I asked Op.

"Nope, he just come out and tore the signs down," Op replied.

Never in my life had I ever quarreled with Jim Wythe. All our relations had been friendly. Then what caused him to do this? Why had he driven six or eight miles out of his way to tear down the signs around my farm that the state had put here to make it a game preserve? No wonder I had heard guns. Men driving by looked my unposted land over. There were not any houses close. This was a fine place to drive their cars in, park beside the road, and hunt without permission. No wonder I had had such trouble last Sunday with a hunter I found in my back yard. No wonder I heard guns on Seaton Ridge and in Sulphur Spring Hollow. And I thought about the lone doe I had seen on this farm. I wondered if some hunter had killed her.

"Yes, Enic Borders come out here and asked me about the sign on the tree in my yard," Old Op said. "I told him what happened. I told him how I had come out of the shack when I heard shooting in my yard. That ornery Jim Wythe didn't know I was home. When I came out, he had shot the sign down. I put him out of the yard. Then he got in his car, drove down the road, and stopped long enough to shoot each sign down. He wasn't drunk either, for he doesn't drink. He wanted to tear something up, for he is a man of destruction. Ever see people like that? Kill game and leave it when they don't want to eat it. Set fire to timber to watch people fight fire. Lay rocks in the road to try to bust automobile tires. They will lay cinders on T-rails to wreck trains. There are people hell-bent on destruction! Well, this Wythe is one of those fellows. I told him to get out and stay out.

"Then, I walked to Greenup," Old Op continued, "and had a man to call Borders. After he got the call through, I did the talking. I told Borders plenty. He come down here in a hurry and went to Wythe's home and arrested him. Think that fellow has a wife and three small children. He arrested old Jim and put 'im in jail. Somebody went his bond and got him out of the jail. Old Jim is really in for something. I know he's out of jail for he come back to see me. He tried to get me not to swear against him. But I'll be there in court to swear against him. I have never been a man to destroy. I'm against all that stuff. Let us take what we need and leave something for the other fellow who is our neighbor and for the young people coming on. You never hunt and kill. You try to preserve something for the next generation. Well, some people could take a lesson from you and . . ."

"Thank you, Op," I interrupted.

I asked Op to come in but he said, "No, I'll watch that end of the farm for you until Enic Borders gets here with more signs. I've never seen so many hunters as we have this year. Beats anything I have ever seen. Well, I must get going. Enic will be back with the signs by the time I get there."

I watched Old Op go back down the road in his bright red suit. Long wisps of his gray locks came from under the red tam that tilted forward on his head.

This is hard to believe, I thought. I never dreamed Jim Wythe, who is supposed to be my friend, would be a destructionist.

Then, I thought: "There are really only two classes of people in any country in the world. It doesn't matter about their religion, color of skin, or political ideas as much as whether or not they are builders or destroyers. People all over this entire world are either constructionists like Old Op, or destructionists like Jim Wythe."

As for me, I never hunted myself, but I raised game on my farm. The game raised on my farm, which I helped protect, didn't stay but went off onto other farms where it was hunted and killed. I had bought seed with my own money and planted crops to feed this game. The state had posted this land for a game preserve. Yet, a man came to tear down the signs so hunters would invade this game preserve! So, maybe one had shot the doe I had found in my pasture. These destructionists would do anything. They would not stop as long as they could be benefited personally. And many wouldn't stop destroying even when they did not benefit in the least from what they destroyed. They destroyed for the fun of destroying. They got some sort of synthetic thrill by tearing down instead of building. And strange to think, when you measure up the people you know in your present day community, you will find that many of them are destructionists. Make a survey of your own community and you will see.

Go back into the history of nations from the early dawn of history until our present time. We have always had two kinds of leaders—the destructive and the constructive. And when you think back to the well-known, highly popularized leaders, you will find it easier to select a list of great destructionists than to select a list of great constructionists.

One of the six greatest destructive leaders was Alexander the Great, who, three centuries B.C., conquered the known world and cried because there were no more lands to conquer. Yet because this man destroyed, he was called Great when he captured and made slaves of one-eighth of his world's population. He destroyed cities, farms, bridges, highways. Historians through the ages have glorified him by calling him Great. Because he is a glorified destructionist he has become a school boy's dream in this modern day world.

Then came Genghis Khan, 1162-1227, one of the most cruel of all the world's great destructionists. Since he was Oriental he has not been idealized too much by young Occidentals of this Western world. He destroyed Asia and threatened Europe before a natural death ended his hopes and dreams of further destruction. He, perhaps, retarded the progress of civilization five hundred years. When we studied about Khan, the destructionist, centuries later in our high school in America, our teacher laid his barbaric cruelty to the fact that he lived so many centuries ago. Even then, I disagreed with my teacher because our greatest constructionist were born centuries before him.

Then came Napolean I, who retarded the progress of civilization another two centuries. In his heyday of power, Europe was an armed camp. Man power had to be utilized by nations to protect their boundaries or their countries would have perished. All Napoleon knew was to invade, kill, destroy, and conquer. He knew the art of killing and plundering. And for his proficiency in both of these destructive arts, instead of being ignored and forgotten, he has been honored by his having more books written about him than any other man in world history. The heroes for our young have certainly been false up through the centuries of our existence when a man who should have been hanged by the neck has been idealized in book, song, and movie for almost a century and a half following his world debacle.

As a race, the early Spaniards deserve to be mentioned for, in the name of God, they didn't leave a native to tell the sad story or write the history of the Island of Cuba. In the name of God, they slaughtered the Indians in the American West. In the name of God, they shot them in Mexico and in South America. Other people shot them, too, but they had enough mercy to leave a few. Others had the same quality of mercy of a few of our hunters today who will shoot all the quail in a covey but two or three. But like the Spaniards, we have present day hunters who brag about killing every quail in a covey. To kill, kill, kill man or bird, how can an individual or a race be anything but destructionists?

We thought people of the dim and distant centuries past were less civilized. But what about this? In our time comes Adolph Hitler, who rose to power over many people who detested him and who, basically, are and have been a great and intelligent people and a great race. This man tried to exterminate a race among whom were the world's finest people. He caused the death of six million innocent men, women, and children. This puny, little, fanatical-minded man tried to obliterate a race because he, one man, personally disliked it. He caused a world war and the death of some thirty million. He set the progress of this world back a century. He put an unfair blemish upon the people whom he controlled. He not only hurt the people of the country he controlled but hurt all the Christians in this world because he supposedly was one. In the history of destructionists, he might go down as the Destructionist of Destructionists, and the one who, we hope, will make them unpopular forever. Maybe, with Hilter, the hero worship of destructionists will stop.

Then came the Trinity of Destructionists—Lenin, Trotsky, and Stalin who tried, and partly succeeded, to sell their philosophy of totalitarianism to the world. They now have the world in balance. They sell with the promises of a better life for the underprivileged. All the peoples of the world today know about these men, who are all dead but who have passed their philosophy on to their successors. Everybody in the half of the world's population they dominate has to agree with their philosophy. In elections when only one man runs, everybody had better get out and vote for him.

Our own Western world has not been conducive to producing a great destructionist. Yet one who was heading for great heights was dethroned in Argentina. Juan Peron, the Western world's greatest destructionist, was, at last, ousted.

There are destructionists from Peron to the men like Jim Wythe, who tore down the state's posters around my farm. The destructionist is the man who steers his car out of course to hit a chicken, a dog, or a cat—or to crush a slow-moving terrapin trying to cross the road.

For the battles between destructionists and constructionists the greatest written record is in the Old Testament. Since Cain and Abel and the Garden of Eden, we have had both groups with us. We shall always have them. But if our world is to exist, and if we are to progress, the constructionists must win over the destructionists.

What would our world have been without these leading constructionists—to mention only six of our great ones from the millions who have fought to make the world a better place? We are lucky to have as fine a world as we have after the destruction wrought by some of the leading characters in it. Had it not been for these, we would not have had this world.

Moses led people out of bondage. Moses, the great law giver, changed the world. His laws became the laws of other people, too. No one great man belongs to one race or one country. A man's influence, either good or bad, influences the world. Moses influenced the world for good.

Jesus Christ had the greatest profound influence for good on the world of anyone who ever lived in it. For his greatness, his good deeds, his teachings, for his great constructionism for centuries to come and his influence over a third of the world's people who were later to follow his teachings, he paid the price of death by a jeering, bloodthirsty mob of destructionists. We would need no other philosophy for the world if his teachings were carried out. He said it. He did it! And ironically enough, he had come and finished at the age of thirty-three, the same age of our school boys' hero, Alexander the Great.

If I were to mention any one race of people who have come nearer than any other race to being constructionists in this world, within a split second and without equivocation, my answer would be the Greeks. They went into battle reading poetry. Their majorities didn't want to fight. They had to fight to protect themselves. If their Republic had been left alone, I wonder how much more influence this great and talented race would have had on our world than it has already had. They gave us giants in freedom's way of life.

They gave us too many giants to mention here. They gave us drama, poetry, history, sculpture, philosophy (the basis, after thousands of years, for all of today's great philosophy), mathematics, oratory, law, and science. There isn't anything connected with the arts they didn't touch. This small minority race had a way of life which has influenced the world through the centuries. Our world progress would be retarded greatly without the influence of the Greeks on civilization. For Greece's great gifts to the world, she was virtually destroyed. But what she gave the world could never be, and has never been, destroyed.

Abraham Lincoln eradicated slavery in our northern hemisphere of the Western world, and he kept men free in this part of the world. He held his divided country together. He was the greatest constructionist that ever came from our Western world. And he must rate with the ten top constructionists of the world. He paid for his good work with a bullet in his brain.

A constructionist many of us have lived to remember was Mahatma Gandhi. Without force and bloodshed, this wisp of a man was leader of approximately one-sixth of the world's population. He had admirers from all over the world, from all religious groups, because he struggled to uplift troubled humanity, among whom his own people were the most troubled. This saintly, great constructionist paid, too, for his making the world a better place to live by having his life snuffed out by an assassin's bullet.

David Ben-Gurion, out of necessity for his

persecuted people, had dreams of an Israel, a land by tradition and history his people owned. This was his dream. And by his hard work and with cooperation from others, Israel was born, a mecca for a race of people that has suffered at the hands of dictators and despots. Their country was the last country formed in this world on rocky, barren, arid soil, worn out centuries ago. They are making fruit trees, timber, grass, grain, and vegetables grow. David Ben-Gurion is a constructionist who is saving people and land and bringing back fertility to impoverished soil, and plant, and animal life. He is re-establishing what ruthless, ignorant destructionists have destroyed.

Albert Schweitzer, philosopher, musician, doctor, man of God, and man of many talents, was one of the great constructionists of our time. He could have had personal wealth and glorification in Europe if he had chosen to remain there. Instead, he submerged his own life and gave his talents to the underprivileged of a shadowy spot of our dark continent, Africa. But he could not completely submerge his talent, for it shone like a lonely star on a dark night for a whole world to see.

But how many books are written about Moses, Jesus, Lincoln, the Greeks, Gandhi, Ben-Gurion, and Schweitzer to make them popular to youth over the world as compared to the exploits of Alexander the Great, Genghis Kahn, Napoleon, Hitler, Lenin-Trotsky-Stalin (for the teenagers of the Oriental world), and Juan Peron?

Youth like to read of the exploits of these men, who have been written about so often in books, magazines, and newspapers. They dream themselves into one of these characters, leading vast armies and conquering the world. It is because men pattern their thinking on destructive models that the minister, the priest, the teacher, the policeman, the fireman, and the game warden—those among us who try to make the world better in thought and deed—are the subjects of jokes and are often looked upon in disdain by people of the community who are destructionists at heart.

We have the destructionists with us. They have been with us since the beginning of recorded time. They will be with us until the last of time is recorded. Everybody on this earth is one or the other. You are either on one side or the other. And these groups are in every country and nationality on this earth. There is a never-ending war between them—and there will never be a truce. This war is not just on my farm between a fellow named Jim Wythe and me. Jim Wythe delights in the destruction of posters warning hunters my farm is a game preserve. This very tug of war is going on now in every rural community, city, town, county, state and country. There is ever that continuous fight. And this fight will go on forever.

For my giving permission to my state and my cooperating with conservationists so we might help those of the future, I am called many unpopular names. And I do not hunt any wild game, but feed and care for it for others to kill when it leaves this farm. I am criticized because I have millions of trees and set more. I will not use these trees. Others will. But fires have been deliberately set and my trees have been killed. Maybe by one who hasn't anything personally against me but who is one of the world's destroyers. I have fought for the morals of humanity, for honest and clean government without thinking of pay or an office. I have fought for land conservation and other constructive conservation practices. I have backed these physically and spiritually and in any other way I could for people of all kinds and for our country. I would back such for other countries. For we know now one country can almost destroy a world.

We, the constructionists, cannot stand or sit idly by. We must be vigilant. Knocking down hunting signs is only a molehill as compared to mountains before us of better and more honest government and of peace for a world; of, definitely, the preservation of health and morals of our world peoples and of the conservation of all our natural resources which we and other generations will be needing more and more as the years go by.

Now weigh yourself. See if you expect to take and not give, or if you expect to give more than you take, to build instead of destroy. Weigh yourself, and if you want to leave the world better because you have lived, you are a constructionist. If you see yourself at the head of a marching army, obliterating people, applying the scorched earth policy to helpless people, obliterating those you dislike for the thrill of it, supervising a slave labor camp or approving of one, then you are a destructionist. The man who drives out of his course to hit a dog or smash a terrapin on the highway or shoots down posters around a game preserve is another. Now weigh yourself carefully. Which one are you? Which side will you be on in the crucial years ahead?

THE PEOPLE I MEET

Our meeting place is W-Hollow. I do not see the people, not all of them, but this little valley of beautiful W-Hollow is our meeting place. They do not always meet me on my own terms. But our meetings are good. Sometimes the only difference is our points of view.

Now people meet me every day and each of the four distinct seasons of the year. We have strange communications, not big such as men have in business transactions! Ours are small, friendly—for the most part—communications like a bright April wind fingering the tender grasses of my small meadow bottoms along the W-Hollow Stream.

I have met in the past and these meetings continue to increase, people I do not see—and will never see. I meet them through their letters that come to me from countries over most of the world. I've met people, whom I have never seen, from every state in the United States and from our outlying possessions. I've met them year after year by the thousands.

But these very interesting people I've met but have never seen are from Czechoslovakia, Denmark, Germany, France, England, Ireland, Scotland, and Wales—even one from the Isle of Man. From Norway, Sweden, Finland, Egypt, Lebanon, Greece, and Italy. Not many from

Turkey, but from West Pakistan, Bangladesh, India, Syria, Yemen, Qatar, Kuwait. Many from Formosa, Korea, Japan, New Zealand, Australia. And from Africa—Zambia, Tanzania, Kenya, Rhodesia, South Africa, Sudan, Libya, Congo, Morocco, Tunisia.

I've met them from Mexico, Panama Canal, Honduras, Colombia, Brazil, Argentina. Countries in South America have been less communicative with me than from other places where I've had more publications.

I have met them here in W-Hollow from all continents on earth and from all the countries I've mentioned here.

Ninety percent of these communications have been in English. I am convinced my language and the language of W-Hollow is a world language, although I'm not sure it was ever intended to be. I've been told there are many languages much easier to learn than English.

Now, why is W-Hollow our meeting place? Why have they communicated with me? Why have they met me in W-Hollow? It is because over the years and now at the present I've communicated with them. I have met them in their countries before they have met me in W-Hollow. I have met them in their textbooks, schools, libraries—I've met them unknowingly. It is very strange to meet so many people of other lands this way.

After reading of my characters in stories and books, they tell me they have them, too. I know they have. Africa is the richest continent in the world for fresh, untainted literary material. It reminds an imaginative creative person of lush grass growing along the Nile. Material unwritten is everywhere on the African continent. Very little of Africa's material has been or will be written. Much of it will never be written. It is like old winds that have blown out—old winds never remembered—sweeping over the vast continent of Africa and are gone forever.

But what I've sent to countries of other continents has come from my North American continent, and my microscopic area of Kentucky known as Appalachia. What I have written of characters here, of young people, people of all walks of life from young to old, but with special stress on older and more colorful men—characters people of other parts of the world have realized they have something in common with me—people like my people.

In Czechoslovakia, where *TAPS FOR PRIVATE TUSSIE* was a best seller, I was informed they had Tussies, too! They had people who wanted something for nothing and who preferred dancing to work. I'd travelled in Czechoslovakia, but I hadn't observed this. Maybe, I didn't know the country and its people well enough.

Old Opp in *THE GOOD SPIRIT OF LAUREL RIDGE,* who believed in ghosts, was quite a character in Germany. I had not known or had forgotten if I had known, that German literature is filled with folk ghost and supernatural literature. Sure, certain Germans wrote me they had similar characters to Old Opp—so hard to believe in such a modern and highly industrialized nation.

Many from England, Ireland, fewer from Scotland, still fewer from Wales have met me in W-Hollow with their communications! But where did we get our way of life in Appalachia? We have retained much of the culture of these older countries. My characters are mainly British Isle stock.

But why do the French-speaking and Arabic-speaking countries of Africa have something in common and occasionally write me? They have no trouble getting my address. My books have this. Their communications finally reach me in W-Hollow. I doubt that very few are lost in the mail.

There are three bonds between us. That all of us have fathers is the first common denominator. In the Arab world the father is dominant. My father in *GOD'S ODDLING* has reached them in English and in French. Our second common denominator is that the young and most of the middle-aged and even the old are trying to improve themselves educationally. *THE THREAD THAT RUNS SO TRUE*, translated in Arabic, Japanese and French, is used/or was/ widely on the African continent and in the Near East. "Our school problems are like your problems," students and teachers have written me.

Then, there is the third common denominator between peoples in the Arab world and me. This is our love of animals. One of my junior books is *RED MULE*. Red Mule loved mules and tried to keep them from being replaced by tractors. He was a great hero to Arab children and their parents. They knew and loved Red Mule. Many of the fellahin who have farmed the Nile Valley for more than five thousand years and the Bedouins, nomads who live with their herds of sheep and goats, still sleep with their animals. They ask me if there was such a great man as Red Mule! And from W-Hollow I send them communications that there was a Red Mule. And there certainly was.

It's unfortunate that Red Mule of Greenup County, U.S.A. couldn't have been born among these people who will never let the tractor replace their donkeys. Had Red Mule been born there as an Arab he would have been worshipped. He would have had a great following. He wouldn't have suffered the fate he did in Greenup County. He was living in a big barn with seventy mules he'd gathered with his last money—trying to save them from going to a meat factory up North where they would have been processed into kennel rations with nice labels on the cans. Red Mule was eating mule feed with his mules when he toppled over! Here's the man the Arabs wanted to know about. Who cared for Red Mule here, who let his hair grow long in winter and never shaved his face until springtime when the weather grew warmer? This was before the common practice of long hair and untrimmed beardly faces.

My communications from wonderful Iran, a

literary land, if I have ever found one, has provided me with many communications. I wish all my books—and not just a few—could have been published there. Poetry in this land is dominant. In West Pakistan and East Pakistan short stories and poetry are dominant, but it is still the land where the father is supreme. And, *GOD'S ODDLING,* about my father, was published here. My stories and poems have been published in their magazines. Due to a war between the Pakistans, my communications now are practically nil. With *THE BEATINEST BOY* published in Urdu in India, I've learned by rare communications that everybody has grandmothers, too.

My big common denominator with the peoples of East and West Pakistan, India, Formosa, and Korea—has been my snake stories. These have been in their textbooks. My snakes are W-Hollow snakes, but they fit well among Mohammedans who respect snakes and Buddhists who worship them. Some of my writing about not killing but protectiong wildlife has pleased the Buddhists.

I have found the world a very good place, since citizens so unalike by nationalities, governments, and religious barriers, have some interest in my people, animals, reptiles and birds, and educational struggles and accomplishments from Appalachia of which only a fragment is my W-Hollow, a very small world. With people the world over there are many common denominators.

I go to them first with my words on paper. This is how we first communicate. Then, they write me if they find the communication good. I meet them on their printed page in W-Hollow. And I always return a message to them. I think as I do this, it would be wonderful if there were time enough and health enough for me to meet and talk with them. Yes, never ending talk, getting our countries together under our common denominators and making our lives more compatible with each other on our earth.

Photo by G. Sam Piatt

W-Hollow

THE SIMPLE JOYS

When I arrived in Manila on December 24th, there were lighted Christmas trees all over the city. On our way from the airport to Manila Hotel, our car had to wait at a stop light, opposite a park in which a Christmas pageant, depicting the birth of Jesus, was being held. The shepherds were standing around the Holy Child as He lay in a manger, with His Holy Mother looking down on him. A considerable crowd had gathered around to watch this pageant. After the countries in which I had been traveling, it was very strange to come upon a scene like this.

"How long have Christmas festivities been in progress?" I asked Carol Harford, an assistant in the American Embassy in Manila.

"I don't know," she said. "I've not paid too much attention to it—but for at least two weeks." Then she spoke reflectively: "Does this interest you?"

"Yes, it does," I said. "It seems so strange. I've not seen a Christmas toy where I've been. I've not seen a Christmas tree—then I drop out of the skies down into this new world. I've been among the Moslem, Hindu, Zoroastrian and Buddhist!"

"Well, you're in a Christian country again," she said.

"Yes, I know, I tried to get to the Phillippines for Christmas," I said. "How long will the festivities last? Until the day after Christmas?"

"No, much longer," she replied. "The Christmas trees won't come down until January 7th. The Filipinos are basically Malayans, but they were under Spanish rule for about four centuries and the Spanish converted most of them to Christianity. The Moros in the south are Moslem and we have some Buddhists here, but it's eighty-five percent Christian. Oh, yes, we have pagans, too—in certain areas—especially in the mountains!"

"Catholics are predominant here. However, there are many Protestants—Presbyterians and Methodists."

But now I was in a Christian country—a country that was first a colony of Spain and then an American possession from 1898 to 1946. What would it be like? I had heard so much talk about the Philippine Islands from the time I was a small boy until the present.

Spain, predominantly Christian, and America, largest predominantly Christian country in the world, were showing their religious influence here. The Christmas celebration was greater than I had ever seen in any of the large cities of the United States.

And there were more Christian emblems in Manila than I had ever seen in an American city. There were Christmas trees shaped out of neon lights that flashed on and off on high rooftops. There were crosses made of nonflashing lights and crosses made of lights that flashed on and off to get the attention of the people. There were anchored balloons with Christian emblems floating up high over the city. This was indeed a Christian country.

When I was taken to the Manila Hotel, the lobby of this large hotel was decorated from end to end with Christmas trees filled with brilliant lighting. Every kind of Christmas tree decoration was displayed. People at the desks were whistling or humming familiar carols.

My wife Naomi was with our daughter Jane back in Kentucky. I knew they were happy having Christmas together. Here I had just arrived in this Christian land in time for the greatest of our Christian holidays—Christmas, the birth date of our Lord. Here I had expected to receive Christmas packages from home, but not one had arrived! I didn't know anybody in the Manila Hotel. But I was happy to be here, even if I did have to celebrate Christmas alone.

I had Christmas gifts, too! When I went to my room there was the luxury of a radio which I switched on immediately to see if it would work: It did, and I could hardly believe it. It was only the second time on my tour that I had had a radio that would play. There was also hot water with which to shave and I had a big clean bed in an air-conditioned room. And here I could listen to Christmas music for about all the music I could get on the radio was Christmas carols. It was "Western" music in the same way that Spain is considered a "Western" country because it is far west from here. I'd not heard music like this since leaving America. I had heard wonderful music in

Greece. But Greece had been the only Christian country I had visited since the beginning of this tour.

In my visits to foreign countries where people were Moslem, Hindu and Buddhist, I had respected their rights to their worship for their religious beliefs were part of their cultural heritage. But Christianity was my cultural heritage.

On this Christmas Eve, I had so many things to be thankful for, even if I didn't get a gift from friends back home. Although I am a cardiac, I had kept my health. This was a great Christmas gift. I had not, so far, bogged down on the most strenuous journey in my lifetime, a journey through six countries, speaking on an average of from one to three times per day, besides going to many other functions. I had slept on different beds, had eaten different foods. I had known travel, travel, and travel. I had been on the road constantly meeting new faces and facing different groups and different situations—even where people were hostile to my country, but seldom hostile to me as an individual. I wouldn't let them be hostile to me. While we had talked, we understood each other. Something of my Christian heritage, an innate something deeply embedded in my heart, mind and soul went to work to remove dark clouds and the so-called immovable objects between their people and my people and our countries.

My Christmas was wonderful, for the simple

joys of being in a Christian country, hearing this Christian music and receiving the benefits of Philippine know-how and cleanliness. Here was the "machine of the West," so highly condemned but so badly needed over the world to make life easier and more comfortable! Manila was a modern and beautiful city. I loved Manila. I was doubly enjoying this special Philippine Christmas, which was a great Christmas—the greatest one I had experienced in many years.

THE POETRY OF THE NILE

This morning I am reading a poem. I am on a fast, diesel-pulled, through train from Alexandria to Cairo. The poem I am reading is called, "The Nile's Green Strip at Sunrise." Old Ra-atum, the ancient Egyptian sun god, rises like a big yellow disk on the East side of the Nile and he rolls along at first like a golden Pharaonic chariot wheel. Then, he leaves the green carpeted earth and climbs up bright stairsteps of the wind, up and up but not to the mansions where the ancient Egyptians dwell. They dwell with their Pharaonic kings and queens in mansions below. And many of the other gods are down there with them. Amen Ra, Annbis, Atoun, Hathor, Matt, Min, Isis, Neyhthys, Osiris, Itah, Sobek, Seshet, Sekmet, Thoout and Horus and their servants are down there looking out for their welfare.

Out in the green fields in a peculiarly bright, eerie twilight the fellaheen are out with their hoes digging into the black earth. Men are plowing, their cows hitched to ancient plows. Everywhere are whole families and groups of families and animals of all kinds—asses, buffalos, cows and steers, camels, donkeys, herds of fat-tailed sheep, and Egyptian brown sheep without the fat tails. The fellaheen, the distinct race of soil people, are the foundation stones of Egypt. They have fed their country for more than five thousand years. In their Nile Valley home their hands have touched every grain of fertile earth from the surface of this soil to 80 feet below. Due to the soil deposits of their Father Nile, the land builds up and up. In 4,600 years it has grown 80 feet. All down through the soil that feeds us and that which has fed millions of others, fellaheen hands, so many millions of them, have lovingly and fondly touched soil that fed Egypt yesterday and now.

The mothers are working with their husbands and children. They walk straighter than the palms stand—along the ditches with baskets, pans, and bottles on their heads. Their hands never touch these loads on their heads when they walk gracefully along dressed in their ancient black regalia. Most of the people are barefooted, and what is wrong with this? I came from people of the soil on another continent. I used to go barefooted, and my mother liked to do the same, and often did, but great changes came to our land. But in this ancient land, it is still much the same as it has been.

The white egrets fly over, slicing the strange twilight air that hangs over the fields like an eerie canopy. These birds are called the friends of the fellaheen farmers. They are never molested. They are beautiful; they are periods at the ends of lines of poetry where they stand in the green fields and watch the fellaheen dig with their short-handled hoes.

The wheat is very tall out here. The oats and

barley are tall, too. The tomatoes are turning on the vines. Fronds of the palms swish in the puffs of morning wind; and when the wind moves on to another palm, the fronds that were disturbed settle down very quietly again.

But why should a village, a house, a barn ever mar the beauty of this Nile river poem? And why should death ever call the fellaheen home to the cities of the Dead near the villages? One layer of dead buried upon another? A fellah is never ready to leave this Heaven on earth he knows and loves. No land on earth has ever produced more varieties of fruits, vegetables and grain that grow and bloom and yield under the kind guidance of their strong and durable hands. No land in the world has ever consistently produced more per acre for five thousand years. And no land in the world is as fertile now. Thank you, Father River Nile, for carrying the sediment over endless miles from Abyssinia's volcanic mountains to fertilize this land and to make the good things grow here.

In the distance a fellaheen woman rides an ass along a narrow road that separates two sections of wheat. Following her is a camel walking slowly, with his head up as high as the fronds of a palm beside an irrigation ditch.

A small area of land is flooded with standing water. A barefooted fellah is wading in it. And far beyond, coming through the bright wind over the landscape, are three fellaheen women. Dressed in black, they follow each other along a path through the wheat with jugs on their heads.

Along the strip of road that follows this

canal, a little ass pulls a cart. The cart is loaded with heavy palm fronds. The fellah is walking along beside the cart helping the little animal pull. Out where massive greenness sprang from the deep dark soil, out here in this strange web of poetic life, where people live a simple life, they are kinder to their animals than they are to each other. They have seen these animals born. They have cared for them and loved them from birth. They have lived with them. On cool nights many have huddled against their animals for warmth, for both slept on the ground behind roofless mud-brick walls.

Night after night I hear the carts and wagons rattling down the street in front of our apartment. This street follows the Nile down to July 26th Bridge. Here the vehicles cross over to the heart of Cairo to sell their produce before 4 o'clock in the morning. Egyptians spurn canned foods. And their fresh fruit and vegetables come from the green valley of the Nile.

These loaded carts have come from the farms along the canals up to the Giza Road, and instead of crossing the busy El Tahrir Bridge they turn left and follow the road along the Nile on Gezirah Island. I have stood on the street at midnight to watch them pass. I have seen as many as twenty carts, loaded with cabbages, oranges, tangerines, potatoes, crates of chickens, crates of eggs, tomatoes, bananas, melons, green beans, radishes, and beautiful loads of cauliflower, going to feed a city of almost four million persons. On top of the loaded carts drivers often lay sleeping while their little asses keep in step in the wagon trains.

The creaking wheels in the night, the rolling wagons and carts and the sounds of the animals' hoofs, the talk and laughter of the drivers have become a familiar song that often lulls me to sleep. This is Cairo, the largest city in Africa. These are the fellaheen going by. The fellaheen feed us. They feed the population of Egypt as their ancestors before them have fed countless generations of people. Out there on either side of my fast moving train is poetry written without words. It is the picture poetry similar to that picture language left in the tombs by the Pharaonic Egyptians. Only the picture poetry I am reading—the dark-soil words, the swish of the palm frond, the green wheat's bending and rising in unison when the winds blow over and pass on.

There is the poetry of movement in women, men and animals. What a strange poetic world are these fellaheen and their animals along these green pages of the Nile, where on either side of the green page are the brown pages of Sahara desert sand. Now, our train is moving into the outskirts of Cairo. In the distance the Sphinx looks at us with sightless stone eyes and the lovely sentinel pyramids, silhouetted against he blue morning sky, look down upon a dreamy world of poetic movement of people and animals, and a storybook of green and brown pages—the same as those the people read and loved five thousand years ago, and maybe even two thousand years before that.

Jesse Stuart walking at W-Hollow

A NEW GARDEN OF EDEN?

Greece has a population of nine million on fifty-three thousand square miles of mainland in southeastern Europe and her island possessions in the Aegean and Mediterranean Seas. On the mainland there are rugged mountains and fertile valleys. There are extremely dry areas and there are those in the north in Trace and Macedonia, and Epirus in the northwest, where there is ample rainfall for good crops. In Greece's approximate central area, Thessalia (The Thessalian Plains), there is excellent farmland. Down in the southern area, the Peloponnesus, there are plains of mountains and wet and dry areas. But in portions of the Peloponnesus there are about the best fruit growing and farming areas as can be found in all Europe. Just about the poorest farming area in all of mainland of Greece is found in Attica, an area where over a fourth of the population lives. This area is dry and the soil is not good. Yet, portions of the land produce grain, fruit, and vegetables.

But how long will Greece be able to produce from her native soil to feed her ever increasing population? At the slow rate of population increase, Greece will be able to feed her people for some time to come if the people will observe a few, simple, improved farming practices. They are simple—not expensive—ones the farmers can do while farming their land during the long productive season. By working a few extra hours each day between fruit and grain seasons and practicing soil conservation they could soon double their present production of grain, vegetables, and fruits.

Or they can continue with their bad farming practices and someday in the not-too-distant future, with their ever-increasing population, run into a catastrophic dilemma—one where their land will no longer feed their people.

They can, and had better, decide now which to choose—farm prosperity, with vegetables, grain, and fruit-a-plenty, to feed their population and to export, or they can in years hence live in the years of want, years when they will have to import grains, and perhaps, fruits.

Let me qualify myself. I am an American school teacher, writer, and lecturer who has been sent to Greece because I asked to go there. In view of my feelings about the great intellectual harvest that has been produced in Greece as a country, and especially in Attica, and Athens by Athenian immortals, I have a personal affinity for this great race of people. There is no race of people on earth like the Greeks. There probably will never be another race on earth who will contribute the intellectual harvest and artistic creativity these people have given to the world. Nevertheless, my observations are not to be taken as an affront—nor do I apologize for writing about their farming practices which are destructive in many respects.

I live on a 1000-acre American farm—the land where I was born. Each season I helped my father farm, or farmed myself, as far back as I can remember. Because my father's horse sense knowledge of soil conservation and farming practices, and because of my reading works of American farm specialists and by applying their free advice and help to meadows on which we once grew a hundred bales of hay, we learned to produce five thousand!

Heavier rains fall in Kentucky than in Greece, and the texture of our soil makes it more susceptible to erosion than the soil of Greece. Yet, we don't have an eroded ditch on our one thousand acres. We have prevented ditches, my father and I, with little or no expense and with a few hours labor.

One educated Greek to whom I mentioned the abuses of Greek soil, said, "It's hard to get them to change from the old methods. They are stubborn. They won't do it."

But I do not agree with his reply. I believe if the Greek farmer knew that a few simple, inexpensive farm practices would help him, he would gladly cooperate. Many American farmers, many not well schooled nor with a lot of money to spend, improve their land by simple, inexpensive methods. I believe that soil conservation and farming practices which save and improve land and increase production are among the finest things we can send to a friendly country overseas, especially since American farm know-how exceeds our other fields of scientific advancement. In the crowded and ancient areas people have starved the hungry land—actually "bled it to death." Land has to be fed, too, before it will produce. Giving help through our know-how has more value than our cultural programs—which includes what I am doing. Of course, what I'm doing isn't without value! But eating properly, which produces healthy people, must come first to produce healthy minds and then healthy cultures.

In a discussion with another Greek, he reminded me Greece had been farmed 5,000 years, perhaps 10,000 years, and it was still Greece and the land was producing. The Greek farmer had done a pretty good job of it since Greece was now exporting fruit to Europe, especially Germany. And I reminded him of the high prices we had been paying for food, much more than we paid in America, and that the average wage in Greece wouldn't be one-tenth as much as the average wage in America. I reminded him of the prices I had paid for fruit despite there being so much of it growing in Greece, seventeen cents for a small pear, (20 drachmas for four small pears and the drachmas exchange for three and a third American pennies) and that I had paid at the restuarant across the street from my hotel, three drachmas, or ten cents, for a small hard roll. This to me did not look like abundance of fruit and grain—native Greeks had to pay these same prices unless they knew places where they could buy cheaper. They probably did. I hope so.

In my travels over Greece I observed one of the most abominable farm practices I have ever seen. No one can ever imagine a Dane, German, or Dutchman, in his home country or his adopted country of America, plowing up and down hill. I have never seen this done in America, yet I found this practice everywhere in Greece. It would have been much easier on man and animal if the farmer had plowed with the contour of the slope. I watched carefully to see if the farmer owned only the narrow strip of land up and down the slope, whereas, if he had to plow with the contour of the slope, he would have had many small turns to make on each side of the narrow strip. I was trying to find a reason why he plowed this way. But he plowed a large area—and all plowed up and down the hill.

After the October and November rains—it rained 27 days out of 31 in Greece—what had happened on these slopes was terrifying. The few inches of soil had washed in many places into heaps of dirt at the bottom of the slopes, exposing the barren white limestone rock in the places up and down the slope. Now, these rains had fallen in supposedly dry Attica, where soil and production are at a premium. But this happened all the way from Athens, 43 miles south to Sounion on the southernmost tip of the Cape.

In my three visits to the central and southern Peloponnesus, one visit the summer before last and two visits last October and November, I found the same farm practices of plowing up and down hill—and the washing away of the soil. Despite what was said about Greece's always being farmed, I thought of how poverty stricken Greece would be, if not for the fact that there was a limestone base to this soil, which provides enough soil above the rock to hold roots and enough rain for moisture so that good crops of fruit and grain are foregone conclusions.

But if the few inches of soil are washed away by up and down hill plowing, there is no dirt to hold roots of fruit trees, vineyards, and grain—certainly the deeper the soil, the more moisture will be contained even when rain doesn't fall. Since it is easier to plow around a slope—easier on man and animal—I could not understand why this hadn't been done. To an American who has had to battle with soil erosion this was a matter of simple practice and common sense. Of course, on my land where there is erosion, I either grow sow grasses that hold the soil, or I plant trees.

Now Greek farmers living in Attica and in the Peloponnesus do not have to have anyone from the outside of Greece to tell them about this bad practice of farming. There is a school, the American Farm School at Thessaloniki, where about 300 Greek men are studying modern American agricultural methods, grain, fruit, cattle, poultry—and above all, soil conservation. There is an excellent map there on contour plowing. But will enough of these young men be educated in time to return to parts of Greece and teach others contour plowing?

There is one place in Greece where extensive soil conservation has been carried on from 1400 to 2200 years before America was discovered. This is on the slope of Parnassus Mountain going from Levadeia toward the village of Arachova.

High, high on the slope of Parnassus Mountain, I saw the greatest soil conservation and soil catching practices I have ever seen in this world. The slope which extends north of Arachova and south of Delphi—a distance of approximately four miles—is an area on which farming would never have been attempted by American or other farmers, except, perhaps, Italian farmers.

Here good farming practices go back to prehistoric Greece. And so do the rock walls built around this steep slope, one after another like gigantic fences to hold the dirt made by crumbling rocks at the top of the mountain near the conical peaks. How can a particle of dirt escape? If one stone wall doesn't catch it, there are forty-nine others down the slope that will. And here, despite all the disadvantages of rugged land, fruit and grain production is something unbelieveable, even on a slope where the village cemetery is divided by a series of stone fences in order to get enough dirt to hold and bury the ancient and recent dead, and to hold the roots of the tall, dark, ghostly cypress trees that stand vigil above the farmers and soil conservationists sleeping there. All the Greeks from all over Greece should see what has been done here. The cost of these conservation walls amounted to millions of man-hours of hard labor.

But where the slopes are more gentle, where rain ditches start, there is a simple practice that can stop most of the erosion without all the work of building stone walls. If this land were mine, I could not sleep with my soil washing to the bottom of the hills. First, I would do contour plowing; and then, if rains came and a ditch was started, I would cut the useless shrub known as broom or whin, a third cousin to the pine, which grows on the mountain and hill slopes of Greece, England and Scotland and use it to prevent erosion.

Here in Greece I would lay whin in the ditches with the tops uphill. The needles would catch and hold the dirt when the rains fell again and the eroded ditch would soon be filled. By doing this, I also would be removing the worthless whim. In addition to whin, there are other shrubs of no value growing here, in Greece which could be used to hold the soil. But since I have used the scrub pines growing on my slopes in America to stop erosion, because of the close fingers on the boughs and each finger filled with needles that would serve as a sieve when pressed in the ditch—a sieve to let the water through but hold the soil—I would choose the whin for this purpose since it is so similar to the scrub pine. And wherever I cut a whin, I would plant a cypress, which will grow where a whin will grow, but which would be a tree of value.

As long as erosion can be stopped in this way, it is better than building a stone wall. The stone wall will always be in the way when plowing—and when earth heals over the whin, the whin will decay, and plows can plow over it.

On a slow train trip around the northern part of Peloponnesus to Patras—and on to the western coast by the Ionian Sea—around the towns of Amalios and Pyrogos I visited some of the finest farming land I had ever seen in all of Greece. Here, the northwestern and the west central coastal area, between the distant mountains and the Ionian Sea, was a vast area, perhaps twenty miles more in width—and maybe one hundred miles in length. It was as fine a farming land as I had ever seen in Iowa, Illinois, or Indiana, in America. Here on this vast coastal plains area, a place where plowing with teams seemed a bit archaic in 1962—I observed a greater mistake than plowing up and down hill. Yesterday on the train ride from Athens to Patras, it had rained all day. Now, on this second day, it was bright and sunny; however, there had been heavy rains in this coastal plains area. Streams coming from the distant mountains and flowing across the plains to the sea, were in some places still overflowing their channels. Forests on mountain slopes and trees in the plains areas provided evidence of good rainfall. Everywhere upon this vast, fertile, level land were pools of water standing in low areas.

First, when I saw men plowing I couldn't believe it was true. Yet, it was true—an unforgettably bad farming practice—plowing ground when it is too wet—especially when a warm sun is in the sky, a sun powerful enough to dry and bake this wet land. Each furrow of earth turned over was so wet that it gleamed in the sunlight. We had a rule at home never to plow land when it was wet enough to squeeze a handful of the dirt and it would stick together and form a mudball.

We had known men back home in the valleys

and on the Kentucky hill slopes who had plowed ground too wet. The land pancaked. It became so hard that it was most difficult to cultivate for clods—that it had to be sown in grass for two years or more until "the land could come back." We doctored sick land on our farm by simple remedies—and when land was plowed too wet, it became so sick it had to take a rest. If rain continued to fall on the wet land after the plowing was done, and then the sun came out hours later, the land wasn't hurt—but we never took this kind of chance, to give our land an opportunity to get sick and have to take a rest.

Everywhere on this coastal plains area, men, and one woman, were plowing with one and two horses. I saw only one tractor and water was following the three plows. Water followed in the furrows behind the plows. There was so much mud in the fields, the plowmen were slipping and sliding. One man was plowing barefooted, wading the water and mud. And the bright sun up in the blue Peloponnesian sky was beaming down on the wind-turned furrows like a hot ball of fire. There was not now, nor had there ever been, nor would there ever be, any excuse, even to sow grain early or sow it late, for a soil practice as disreputable as this one. Back home by carefully improving our few level acres by crop rotation, fertilization, and proper plowing, we had increased our good seed from an approximate 25 to 30 bushels per acre, to a peak high of 150 bushels of corn per acre.

We certainly were not the best American

farmers! For there were the youth of our generation, who planned to farm for a livelihood, who were producing more on their acres than the older farmers. They followed with excessive care all the good farming practices known to Americans. They produced from 2,000 to 2,500 pounds of tobacco on soil that used to grow at its peak production only five or six hundred pounds. These young farmers never abused their soil, but doctored sick soil as they would a sick animal. They constantly improved their soil, took care of it as they did their farm machinery.

And each year, with weather conditions permitting, they increased their yields. As I looked over this vast area of Greece, I wondered what our young and old farmers would do with such excellent land if they had it. While over here, men I talked to thought all Americans had to do was plant and harvest, because our soil was so excellent. If they knew in Greece all that we do for our soil in America, how we nurture, feed, and care for it—sweeten it by drainage and lime it when it sours, and never plow it when its wet. We keep our soil healthy. And our good farmers for the most part never permit erosion. Only through supreme technical know-how, the education of our young, and the most up-to-date farming practices in the world, can seven per cent of our population engaged in farming feed 185,000,000 people, besides exporting food everywhere; we can find markets and store the overproduction in bins over the face of America—while Russia with 53 per cent of its 214,000,000 engaged in farming can not properly feed (they admit their shortages) their own population.

We not only improve the acres that we cultivate but we improve acres that we do not cultivate—and never will cultivate in our lifetime. We know our population will increase and future generations will use these acres.

Then, there is another simple practice which Greeks can utilize in two ways. Everywhere they are expanding farming land. On small farms where stones are gathered up by hand from the gentle slopes and piled up in heaps on the fields, these heaps must be plowed around each season. Sometimes they are piled up in useless heaps at the edges of the field. While picking up these stones, why not erect a small stone fence above the field on the slope to catch and hold the continuous movement of dirt that is gradually washed down by rains? The accumulations of this dirt will build a second level of earth, with a deep soil, suitable for grain, orchards, groves, and even for soil for reforestation. It would be simple to do this, as the ancients did, perhaps 5,000 years ago on the steep slopes of Parnassus Mountain.

If a mountain slope belonged to me, I would do something about pasturing goats, something I believe would be far more profitable. This, too, I believe would be good soil practice and even a good project, for the Greek government—one that will pay dividends in the future. I know that Greece imports paper pulp from Sweden, for I watched their freighters being unloaded in Patras Gulf where there is the largest paper mill in this part of the world. But why import all this pulpwood when it can be grown in Greece? Legends and history tell us that the land of Greece for the most part was once a vast forest. If it was forest once, it can be forest again. Also, people tell me the conquerors of Greece, their Ottoman Empire conquerors, stripped their land of trees. They grew more, but in World War II, the Germans and Italians who occupied this country even cut the trees along the streets in Athens. They cut down fruit trees and burned them.

Yet, the Greeks have not been fighting now for 14 years—a short time and yet, where are the young replanted forests growing on the mountain slopes? Well, there is one on a steep mountain slope—a very small but beautiful one between Corinth and Partras in northern Peleponnesus—and there is an excellent one of several hundred acres on a steep slope left of the highway before one reaches Thebes Valley—going from Athens to Thebes. There are other smaller ones. But these replanted cypress, growing stalwart and tall, are proof enough that trees will grow on these mountains. It is proof enough that reforestation, instead of shrubbery and goats, and erosion where there are goat paths, would be more profitable to the Greek economy and actually would give more people work.

So if I owned a mountain or two mountains in Greece, I know what I would do—to the extent of my resources to obtain labor. I would put a first stone wall down at the base of the mountain. Above this, if there were small worthless shrubbery, I would knock it down to fill the low places with the debris of shrubbery and loose stone. And then I would set the slope in trees—or perhaps some of it in orchards and groves down near the foot of the mountain. My stone wall would catch my soil drifting down. But soon the network of interlacing roots from the young growing cypress would form a bulwark against erosion—and would hold this soil.

Then I would go higher upon the mountain, build another wall, cut down shrubbery if it was there, and I'd set trees. I'd continue this process up as far as I could. Any young man in Greece, who will do this now, will have something of value in a short time. Something certainly more profitable than flocks of goats and worthless shrubbery.

And when I suggest this, I am not talking without experience. This is not a pipe dream. Each year on my farm in America, where land is far more difficult to care for than most of the land I've observed in Greece, I have the land planted with grass and trees. The land is cleared of worthless foliage, stones removed and some acres, let us assume $100 value, will be worth five times as much. Where acres are sowed in grass, they become productive. Where they are planted in trees, they grow in value! So, why couldn't this be done in Greece?

Production from the soil of Greece, due to the limestone base, and the excellent climate for fruits and vegetables, could double and treble. This with better farming practices, just a few simple ones, of caring for and nursing back to health, an ancient and loving land that has fed millions through the past milleniums—a soil that has been treated roughly but has endured like the Greek people who themselves have been treated roughly but have endured. With careful hands and plows, more understanding hearts, and re-awakened minds—this land could be rejuvenated into the most productive area of all Europe. Greece could support its own population with plenty and with plenty to spare—could supply its own timber, pulpwood, and could take the fruit market from all the countries in this area. Greece could become a New Garden of Eden.

W-Hollow in the snow

Photo by G. Sam Piatt

THE SIMPLE JOYS OF SNOW

For forty hours the white flakes tumbled from the skies until we had fourteen inches of this fluffy beautiful stuff melled into a blanket over our North-East Kentucky hills. This was a nice, a beautiful snow, which should have made everybody proud since most everyone dreams of a white Christmas. Well, we were going to have a white Christmas this time because the thermometer had dropped to 14 below . . . which is nothing unusual for this snow-belt area of Kentucky because we're approximately, straight as the crow flies, 200 miles South of Canada.

Aida Demirjian, had arrived four days in advance to spend Christmas Holidays. Aida is a young woman from Cairo, Egypt, who had never seen snow until she came to Berea College, Berea, Kentucky. When I used to teach at the American University in Cairo, she was a secretary there and did a portion of my typing for me. Of Armenian descent, her people had fled Turkey during the great massacre of Armenians by the Turks in World War I. They had come south to Egypt, then mandated by the British. A devout Armenian Orthodox Christian in a predominantly Moslem world, I first took note of her honesty when I started to pay her for typing a book. She wouldn't take full payment for a half typed page at the close of the mss. She would accept only halfpay for a half typed page. I found her to be an unusual girl and my wife and I helped her to get to America and to Berea College. But one thing lacking in her education and experiences, was the simple joys to be obtained from snow. She was in our home when the snow began to fall and she looked admiringly on the fluffy crystal flakes that zigzagged softly down as if the air were invisible props trying to hold them up.

Now there was another young lady, Marianthi Coroneau, whom I had taught in American University in Cairo, in three courses. She was now working on her Ph.D. at the University of Kentucky. She was of Greek descent but had been born in Egypt and had lived there all her life. She was none too familiar with snow, its beauties and the joys to be had from it falling like white soft crystals from the low dark skies to join companion flakes that were forming the vast white blanket over our dark winter world. Marianthi, was to arrive two days before Christmas. But the snow was falling and roads almost impassable when she left Lexington, Kentucky. She called me from the bus station in Ashland, Kentucky . . . not to let a beautiful thing like the snow hold up her spending Christmas Holidays with us. So, she came on and my brother-in-law, Whitey Liles, an excellent and careful driver on slick roads took his car which has snow-grip tires, to Ashland to get her. She was three hours late getting to Ashland.

Marianthi had visited us before and only she had included in a thank-you letter to Naomi: "thank you for the molecules of fresh air." I knew the young Greeks, after having taught them at American University at Cairo, after having visited Greece three times . . . spending time there and going over most of the country . . . and after having read so many plays, poems and books by the ancient Greeks . . . I knew something of the Greek thinking . . . their inquisitive minds . . . and had concluded long ago there was no race on earth who had given so much cultural heritage to the world as the Greeks. I had never in all my teaching ever taught young men and women with such inquisitive minds as the young Greeks possessed and Marianthi was one of these who thought nothing of speaking seven languages, and who was one not majoring in languages in America but in English Literature. And to her own surprise had turned in an almost perfect score on mathematics when she took a preliminary examination before entering graduate work.

Marianthi was excited when she got into the car. The snow was falling again. The streets in Ashland leading to the bus station were covered with hard-packed snow where wheels spun and cars went out of the road. My brother-in-law Whitey, who was not a teacher, said later he had never heard anyone who could say more about snow, roads, America, schools and education than she said in the hour it took to drive home. He was surprised that snow could excite anyone so much as it had excited Marianthi Coroneau. "Oh, how I would like to ride in a sleigh," she said. Whitey didn't say anything for he couldn't. He didn't have a chance. When there was an opening between Marianthi's expressed thoughts, spoken in English without an accent, I being her former teacher and who liked to talk myself, filled in the space. Whitey hadn't taught the young Greeks and he'd not visited Greece. He didn't know the background of a people who loved the countryside, the mountains and valleys and the sandy beaches, the ruins of their ancient temples and some modern public buildings more than they liked the confinements of homes. They spent all their spare time in Greece and some of the time when they should have been working, visiting temples, beaches, in this peninsula and island country where one can scarcely get away from the sound of the sea. Although Marianthi had not grown up in Greece, where there was snow in winter, she couldn't escape the natural traits of her people and her heritage. Anyone who wrote a thank-you note which included "molecules of fresh air" certainly was excited over the snow.

Whitey Liles, who just listened while we talked, drove over a vast white world into W-Hollow where pinetops were weighted by snow and the dark leafless oaks stood stiffly dark like sentinels on the steep slopes above the valley. The belly of his car slithered over middle-of-the-road snow while the wheels stayed in two white ruts that wound in a zigzagging parallel up the valley to home. Here Marianthi and Aida, who had known each other at American University in Cairo, and who went to Berea College and University of Kentucky, only forty miles apart, embraced each other like sisters. But young women from such individualistic races as Armenian and Greek, had to play a game of give-and-take to be sisters. Each had her room upstairs with only a door between.

Before Marianthi had put her clothes away, she was down looking through the stacks of records. She found Greek records that we had purchased in Athens . . . popular and classical. She played these on the hi-fi and she and Aida danced. If Aida didn't know the Greek dance, Marianthi taught her. Now, Marianthi had left her subject of snow, all its beauties, which Whitey couldn't believe since he had battled driving over and through it 30 miles to and from his work with Ashland Oil and Refining Company. He couldn't see the beauty in a crystal that Miss Coroneau described in a torrent of words.

After the Greek Music and Dance, we ate our Christmas Eve dinner. And after this we talked about our white wonderland and the spirit of Christmas. Naomi and I were disappointed when our daughter Jane called from Cleveland and told us that she and her husband wouldn't be down for Christmas . . . that they couldn't make it in their usual six hours drive since reports on the roads were unfavorable. We had Jane's room, furnished with her books, dolls, pictures and her desk and typewriter . . . just as she had left it when she married and left us. We had it waiting for her and her husband, Julian.

It was near midnight when Marianthi and Aida went up to their rooms and to bed and Naomi and I went to our room to bed. In a few minutes we had never heard such good laughter as we heard between Marianthi and Aida. There were three rooms between our rooms. They had to laugh loudly for the sound to carry so far. Naomi and I lay there in bed listening to their laughter until we found ourselves laughing too. Greece and Armenia, countries in the distant past who had fought one another, were joined tonight in America . . . by two of their very fine representatives. While we lay listening to their laughter we heard them speaking in a language, which we couldn't interpret but could identify when spoken, Arabic. Maybe they were enjoying speaking in Arabic again. Then we heard them speaking in French which we didn't understand either.

The loud talking in foreign languages and laughter hadn't subsided at two in the morning when our telephone rang. I knew it was some emergency. I jumped out of bed and answered. The call was from Jane. She and Julian had driven within five miles of home and couldn't get the rest of the way due to ice-coated roads. They had found a roadside pay station from which Jane had called. Then, I phoned Whitey to come with his car with the snow-grip tires. Whitey was in bed but he dressed and came and we went after Jane and Julian. Now everybody got out of bed and waited while Whitey and I went after Jane and Julian. We had them park their car near a filling station where we traded. They brought only a few belongings and got in the car. They were very, very tired. "We got along very well over the Northern Ohio roads," Julian said. "We ran into all this snow in Southern Ohio and Northern Kentucky! This year at Cleveland we've seen plenty of snow."

"Don't you think it's nice?" I said.

"Well, yes . . . in a way . . . if you don't see too much of it," he replied.

"Miss Coroneau and Miss Demirjian won't agree with you," Whitey said.

"Oh, are they here," Jane said. "I'll be glad to see them."

"Yes, they had been in bed," I said. "But they were getting up when I left."

"They're crazy about snow," Whitey said. "They're really enjoying this snow."

When we reached home Jane greeted her mother, Marianthi and Aida and introduced Julian to her friends from Egypt. Now, Naomi made coffee and set food on the table.

"Whitey, you won't get any sleep," I said.

"But I won't be alone," he said. "No one else is getting any sleep. I'm not even going to bed after I go up to the house. So, I'll have a cup of coffee and stay a few minutes."

While we sat at the table eating cake and drinking coffee, Whitey said: "Miss Coroneau, you said today when we came from the bus station you wanted to take a sleigh ride. Now, I've got an idea! I'm going to see that you get a real sleigh ride!"

"On a sleigh pulled with horses?" she spoke quickly.

"No, pulled by a tractor," he said. "What about you, Julian . . . you and Jane! You'll have time to sleep and rest some since I can't take you on this ride before tonight. See, I'm called out to work today!"

We're going to Logan, West Virginia to see Julian's parents this afternoon and we'll spend tonight there and then return here for a day on our way home to Cleveland," Jane said. "Sorry, Uncle Whitey, we'll miss the sleigh ride."

At three Christmas morning Whitey went home and we went to bed. At nine we were up and had breakfast and opened the Christmas packages. Although our home has a central heating system, we have four fireplaces, left-overs from our former heating system. I built a wood fire in one of them which gave us light and cheerfulness while we looked at presents and laughed and talked. Life was wonderful here this morning as we looked from our windows upon the white wonderland of W-Hollow.

"We Armenians have our Christmas on January Sixth," Aida said.

"But we Greeks have our Christmas on December 25th," Marianthi said. "Oh, the beautiful snow;" she sighed as she looked from the window. "I used to hear your song in Egypt, 'I'M DREAMING OF A WHITE CHRISTMAS.' I'm not dreaming of it now. I'm having my first white Christmas! And, I used to hear in Egypt your song, "JINGLE BELLS.' Oh, I remember, it went something like this, she sang:

"Jingle bells, jingle bells, jingle
all the way,
Oh what fun it is to ride in a one-horse
open sleigh!"

"You'll be riding on a sleigh tonight, Marianthi," I said.

The morning passed too swiftly and there was too much food. Breakfast and Christmas dinner came too close. But Jane and Julian couldn't leave on their extended drive into West Virginia mountains another 100 miles, until they had eaten Christmas dinner with us. Then after Christmas dinner, Ben Webb came to deliver and to receive gifts and he took Jane and Julian to their car. At about six Whitey came driving up the valley on his way home from work at Ashland Oil Refinery. He stopped to tell us to be ready for the ride by eight.

At eight o'clock we were ready. Marianthi was bundled, her head wrapped in a scarf. Her slippers covered with galoshes and she was wearing her own winter coat and mittens, plus a winter topcoat of mine which came to her ankles as she was not very tall. Aida who was some taller was bundled in her own winter clothing, plus another topcoat of mine. My wife, Naomi, had seen to it that they were properly dressed to sit and ride on a sled in the deep snow in the sub-zero weather.

When we heard the tractor chugging down the valley we went out on the porch and waited for Whitey to arrive. The big tractor was hitched to a sled which was twelve feet long and approximately five feet wide. We had made the sled of wood. There was a floor but no bed walls alongside or crosswise. Snow was as deep as the sled was high. My youngest sister, Glenna, was sitting on the backseat which was made of two bales of hay. Beside her sat their nine-year-old daughter, Ethel Ann and three-year-old daughter, Lissa.

"Aunt Naomi Deane, I don't want to ride," Lissa said. "I want to stay with you and sing. I want to stay before your fire!"

"All right, Lissa," Naomi said. "We'll stay here."

"Oh, Mrs. Stuart, you'll miss the ride like this?" Marianthi said. "You'll miss all the beauties of this snow. You'll miss the joy of snow, Mrs. Stuart!"

"But I have had the flu," Naomi said. "And maybe it will be better that Lissa and I stay here!"

"Well, Miss Coroneau and Miss Demirjian, the front seat is for you," Whitey said. "I want you up front so you can see and enjoy the snow. You're going to get plenty of this snow that you like so well!

There were a half-dozen blankets on the sled. Marianthi and Aida sat on a bale of hay up front. They put the blankets over their shoulders and around them. Glenna, Ethel Ann and I took the backseat and put the blankets over our shoulders and across our laps. We had Ethel Ann between us.

"Well, have a good time," Naomi said. "Lissa and I will go sing. We will go sit before the warm fire!"

"Everybody ready," Whitey said. "We're off in the snow!"

Whitey pulled away from the road over into

the meadow where the blanket of snow was deeper. It didn't matter if the snow was deeper than the sled was high for the big tractor pulled us through the deep and deeper snow. Some places there were drifts that we sliced through like a knife cuts hot butter. Whitey stood up and drove the tractor. He knew about where the small streams were, now frozen over and snowed under. He wanted to miss these. There was no wind blowing deep in W-Hollow. The stars were dim in the sky above and the moon was full over this vast white world. Even the oaks that had stood stiffly dark on the slopes were frosted white now and looked like ghosts of trees standing sentinel over the treeless valley. Marianthi and Aida's shouts and laughter drowned the chugging tractor that seemed to be laughing in spurts as it pulled us over the snow.

Whitey made a serpentine track down the valley and Marianthi weaved and Aida rocked on their haybale seats. They put their arms around each other and hung on for dear life while Glenna and I put our arms around Ethel Ann and held on too. And we held Ethel Ann snugly between us to keep her from falling.

"Oh how wonderful is snow," Aida said.

Just about this time when Whitey started to leave W-Hollow for a tributary and a lane road where my oldest sister lived, he made a sharp turn and off Marianthi and Aida went into the snow, blanket wrapped with only their faces visible in the moonlight and their wild laughter along with the tractor's chugging laughter broke the stillness of this Christmas night. They just lay there in the snow and laughed. Whitey stopped the tractor. He got off and helped them back on while they laughed, dipped their mitten hands into the snow and threw the fluffy beauty into the air. Since we had almost tumbled I put our haybale seats back in order and rearranged our blankets. Now everybody got seated and we were on our way, not up the road, but up a bottom filled with deep snow and up across a garden where my sister, Sophia and brother-in-law, Henry lived. Whitey ran around the house and had tractor and sled heading back down the valley then he stopped suddenly.

"We'll pay them a call here," he said.

My sister and brother-in-law, had perhaps never met an Armenian and Greek. Certainly they had never met them at the same time. And they were delighted when we paid them this unexpected visit. We went in with the girls and introduced them. Sophia and Henry offered us food but no one touched it. We'd been having food all day. And the table was filled at home. Anytime after mealtime when one of us wanted more turkey it was on the table for us . . . turkey and a dozen other things. But each of us, except little Ethel Ann accepted a cup of hot coffee. Henry and Sophia, who had four children, three daughters and a son, married and gone from home were fascinated by Miss Coroneau and Miss Demirjian. They laughed loudly when Marianthi lapsed into a descriptive interlude on the beauty of snow under the moon, something unknown in her native Egypt. "Oh, the little grains are good to touch and feel," she said. "It feels good but cool against the face." Our visit was a delightful one.

"Sorry we have to leave you," Whitey said. "But we've got to be on our way. We've got places to go."

After saying our farewells, we went back to the sled. We took our seats and wrapped blankets around us. Whitey started the tractor and we were on our way. The big wheels kicked up a storm of dry fluffy snow that shone like grains of polished silver in the moonlight. These bright soft flakes came back and hit Marianthi's and Aida's faces. Loose snow showered us on the backseat like white raindrops. I was beginning to agree with Marianthi that there were simple joys to be had from snow. This evening we were enjoying these simple joys. Whitey had now reached the mouth of this small nameless W-Hollow tributary. He was back on the W-Hollow road which he had to follow. We followed the road which was parallel to the ice-bound creek. At Dead-Man's curve, my small sister couldn't hold her large brother and I rolled off, haybale and a blanket into the deep snow while everybody laughed and I did too. Whitey stopped and I put my seat back and got on and wrapped up in the blankets.

We stopped when we reached the top of a small hill at Check and Viven Lowe's. Viven, was Henry's and Sophia's second daughter. When we stopped there was no one home, although they lived on the W-Hollow road their house was unlocked and we went in. There was coffee made and left on the warmer and the table was filled with food but we didn't bother the food nor the coffee. Had we been able to have eaten we would have. So we went back to our sled.

"Now, get ready for the big hill," Whitey said. "We're going to a high windy place. We're going up to the stars!"

"How are we going up there?" I asked.

"Right up through the cemetery," he replied.

Three Mile Cemetery, a pioneer cemetery, held many of our pioneer dead. There was a road up through this cemetery most of which was now overgrown with large trees. The road that went up here, went back to a portion of my farm which lay north of this cemetery. In summer this portion of the farm, the flat hilltop and the slopes both east and west, was in meadow and was very beautiful.

When we left W-Hollow road, I thought the front of the tractor should have been weighted for it looked like it was standing on its end. Halfway up, Glenna and I felt our haybale seats slipping toward the rear and we held on to Marianthi and Aida. They slid back too and the five of us had to stop the tractor which perhaps had then enough momentum to carry us to the top. He helped get ourselves and blankets untangled and haybales back in place. When we were seated again, Whitey had trouble. The tractor's wheels spun. They spun down through the snow to the earth. Here they held and pulled us a few feet and spun again. But Whitey, an expert driver with tractors, bulldozers and heavy trucks, zigzagged the tractor slowly but surely until we reached the top.

Here began one of the most beautiful rides I have ever taken. Up here the moon seemed closer to the earth and the stars were brighter. Up here the wind sighed among the barren oaks in a grove on our left. These oaks were frozen stiffly and they were white with frost. When the wind sang among the trees, Marianthi said: "The ghosts are singing." And the ghosts were singing. "I can almost reach up and touch a star," Aida said. "But there is too much snow in my eyes to see stars plainly." The dry snow in powdery sheens was flying back from the tractor wheels as the tractor pulled us over the level ridgeline of snow. And up here on this hilltop were deep drifts but these didn't matter to us. But, had the tractor quit on us, I wondered how we would get back to the W-Hollow road and the warmth of a house.

Up here we traveled a mile along this ridgeline. In the far distance we could look down on the lights in the Ohio River Valley. We could see the lights in the little town of Greenup. Here, I had cleared the waste material from beneath the trees and sowed a meadow. I had cut and baled hay under the trees. Now we were among these ghostly trees looking up among them at the blue sky and blinking stars while over to our left was the magnificient moon. Whitey circled among the trees, dodging and changing course until we came to the end of the ridge. Here, he turned the tractor and we began our journey home.

Instead of following the road back through the cemetery, over which we had broken a road, Whitey chose an unbroken field, of snow. He took us straight downhill toward Gene Darby's home. Gene was my second sister, Mary's, son. Going down this hill everybody tumbled off because Whitey had mown this meadow slope and he knew where he was going. He took us at good speed downhill. At Gene and Hilda's home we learned Hilda, Gene's wife who was from Germany had gone to the hospital with a slipped disc in her back. Gene was gone too. But Gene's mother, my sister Mary was there caring for their two children. Here, there was central heat and a fire in the fireplace too.

After our introductions, Mary offered us hot coffee and food. We refused the food but drank a cup of hot coffee. Here Marianthi and Aida, speaking of splendor of snow and the magnificent beauty of each "tender" flake were looked upon as long-lost friends from faraway Egypt by my sister, Mary, who too, all her life had loved winter and the beauty of snow. Mary said there was nothing she would like to do more than to join us but she couldn't leave her grandchildren. We didn't expect her to, but we would have liked very much to have had her with us.

After warming our hands and feet before the open fire, we waded back through the kneedeep snow to our sled. "I want to ride with them, Mama," Ethel Ann said. "They get more of the "beautiful snow in their faces and they fall more. Mama I want to fall with them. I don't care if they fall on me."

"Come on Ethel Ann," Aida said. "Ride with us."

Marianthi and Aida put Ethel Ann between them and covered her with blankets. Then, we were on our way. We had traveled approximately four miles. Now we had approximately two to go. We had been on my farm all of the way for it lay on either side of the road. The only land not in my farm but in the family farm was Henry's and Sophia's garden. My inlaws and I owned the valley so we could ride anywhere we pleased. We could love the snowflakes and the moon and stars. There was no one to object to where we went or how much noise we made. When Whitey made a serpentine route back up the valley, over a new level of undisturbed snow, Aida, Ethel Ann and Marianthi went from the sled into a snowbank with blankets and haybales covering them. Ethel Ann, small for her years, didn't cry. She laughed hilariously with Marianthi and Aida.

"Mama, I fell too," she said. "It's wonderful to fall in the snow!"

She stood up and brushed the snow from her coat, mittens, and parka.

"This beautiful, wonderful snow in Kentucky," Marianthi said. "I love every little crystal drop! There is joy in the soft blanket made from the fluffy crystal! What a wonderful world this is! I have never had a better time in my life!"

They put the haybales back on the sled and put Ethel Ann between them. They wrapped the blankets around and over them until only their eyes and a little of each face was visible. And we were on our way over the last meadow home. We could see the lights from the home that awaited us. As our long sled skimmed over the smooth white wave, I heard Aida say to Marianthi:

"This is my best Christmas!"

"My best Christmas too and a white one," Marianthi said.

CONSCIENTIOUS ACCEPTORS

It took cold winds, a frost, and near freezing temperatures to convince old terrapin that he had to give up going around under a protective shell, heavier than his body on four weight-bent legs—and his little tail stuck out behind, with his head thrust up into the wind on his long neck—his hard bone lips, and his little beady black eyes. Yes, give up the spring-summer season and get under the ground for his long sleep.

This long rest and sleep wouldn't be anything for old terrapin. For a very long time he has had to be a good conscientious acceptor. If he hadn't been he and his tribe wouldn't be around. Of course, he hates to leave the green nourishment for he is a vegetarian. He lives now in a world not made for him. But this good old slow-going lazy fellow, a good old conscientious acceptor, is about as ancient as anything that walks or crawls over the land. He goes back, perhaps, as long as geological time is recorded—back to the suppositions between the Archean and Paleozoic ages—back where few fossils are found. Maybe, he goes back to the Paleozoic age. He's an old fashioned living thing in an age of automobiles, jets, and missiles. And the reason he's here, surviving over all the ages, is he conscientiously accepts. He knows with the weight of his protective shell he inherited from ages past, a shell not protective now—but how can he eliminate it?—he knows he can't go out and be progressive and turn a bit of earth over to see what's under it. Instinctively, he knows that time has come for him to get down in the earth. His life span can be as long as four human life spans if each is three score years and ten! But we, unlike the terrapin, are more conscientious objectors than we are conscientious acceptors. We never stop trying to out-progress progress! We over use our bodies and wear them down and out!

But old terrapin has friends that go along with him. They, too, are conscientious acceptors. If they weren't they'd have long been extinct from this earth and their images might be found a hundred thousand years hence in fossils.

Yes—and, maybe, they came from the age of antiquity that gave birth to the terrapin! But what about the reptiles? They came somewhere between Ordovician and Paleozoic! And we have to believe—we know they are conscientious acceptors! Have you ever seen a black snake in the snow? If you took one from a warm cage and put him there he'd go to sleep immediately and freeze to death. But let the cool winds of late summer touch him and he knows instinctively that his good days from resurrected spring—crawling over the land foraging for food, frogs, young rabbits, birds, mice, ground squirrels and rodents—all these wonderful days are now in the past, behind him. He will leave no written records of his escapades except his writing tracks on the soft loams and sands. But he knows to find a hole away from freeze where he can go to sleep—and not be awakened until the warm spring rains soak down to him to warm his wrinkled old skin and awaken his reptilian brain.

So we have the reptiles—blacksnake, viper, watersnake, copperhead, rattlesnake, and beautiful little insect-eating green snake—and all are conscientious acceptors. They have survived the ages! They have come down to us! We know they have survived the ages for reptilian forms are found in fossils.

Reptiles—strange long things with forked tongues and lidless eyes—that crawl over earth on scales for feet and legs—with these they crawl and climb. A blacksnake can move at a very fast speed. He can outrun a forest fire if its not burning up a steep hill! Think of how the reptiles have had to be conscientious acceptors to survive in this North Temperate Zone where they have had to spend approximately one half of their lives in cold-blooded sleep somewhere under the ground. Often they endure on scanty food—but they manage to live and reproduce their species from age to age under the most adverse and difficult circumstances.

Another little friend that lives in our yard dates back, perhaps, with the reptile and the terrapin. He is the lizard. And it's very hard for the lizard to be a conscientious acceptor. He's very sneaky about it. If he feels the cold winds he gets very sleepy. And he's likely to go to sleep. But cold winds speak to him. He finds that hiding place! But after he has found that hiding place, if the sun shines warm and brings our a few flies and insects, the lizard will come out too! And he'll feed on flies and insects!

What a pretty little thing the lizard is! I call him a thing—a living thing—I cannot call him an animal or a reptile. He has four legs that can run on the ground or climb a tree at full speed. He has a long tail that tapers. He has a white throat and the small reptilian head. But he doesn't have the forked tongue of the reptile. He has a long, red tongue that can shoot from his mouth and capture a fly in a split second. And, believe it or not, the information I have is that the lizard is akin to the alligator. And the species from this family date back to the Paleozoic period—to the dawn of first discoveries of remains found in fossils—to the dawn of creation!

I make the comparisons of these living forms around me now—I see in my yard—in late spring, summer and early autumn. Lizards live from insects; so does the beautiful greensnake—the only reptile I know that does. Female lizards lay eggs. So do the terrapins, turtles, and non-poisonous snakes. So close to earth these forms of life, they lay their eggs in earth where the sun will incubate and hatch them. Thus, the sun is their incubator. Terrapins are not the only conscientious acceptors who are vegetarians.

Now this is the strangest of all the conscientious acceptors—a warmblooded wild animal! He has to join the association of those with whom he has no kinship. He sleeps in winter! And he's a warm-blooded animal—and a vegetarian. He lives under our house. He and his mate live under our bedroom. They feed on the grass in our yard and on the hillslopes around our home. They feed on the grain we leave in little piles in our yard for them. They are conscientious acceptors all right. But they are slow to accept! They don't like their fate in life! They eat more and add weight in autumn—a fat that helps sustain them while they sleep. And these woodchucks, with their short legs, broad backs, short necks, and pretty heads with sharp black eyes are energetic, hole-digging animals. They are the most beautiful of all wild animals.

How far back into antiquity the woodchuck goes, I do not know. But I presume he is young in comparison to other members of his society of conscientious acceptors—reptiles, terrapins, and lizards. He is the only warm-blooded animal I know associated with them.

But we have birds that are conscientious acceptors! And birds go back to antiquity! This is hard to believe. Birds may go back to Archean and Paleozoic periods. And, hard to believe, birds may go back to the reptiles. Can you believe reptiles have ever flown—reptiles with feathered tails? Birds with reptilian characteristics?

We never knew these birds. But their remains have been found in fossils—the Archaeornis bird. This one, the oldest bird known to man—had the long feathered tail. This bird had the reptilian characteristics. It didn't have a beak. But it had jaws and teeth. And it had teeth on its wings and three free digits with claws—not to our knowledge did one of our human species ever see it. But this was a bird—the earliest one we have ever known. Now we have, perhaps, its descendents, the conscientious acceptors.

But there are birds associated with these. And all birds I know are warm-blooded—extremely warm-blooded. You think of a little feathered bird only a few ounces in weight—that can roost out in vines or evergreens when the weather is subzero and its little heart, its bloodstream, and its coat of feathers can keep it warm sitting in subzero temperatures through the night. And so many of the warm-blooded birds live here throughout the winter. These are not the conscientious acceptors. If anything, they are the conscientious objectors.

The birds that are the conscientious acceptors, and for a very good reason, are the Virginia Flycatchers, peewees, and humming birds. These birds certainly have their warnings. And they do not hibernate and sleep for the winter. They fly away. They leave old habitats and return in another season. It is very interesting how they leave and return to the same place in spring to build new nests!

Can you imagine a Virginia Flycatcher or a peewee's staying around until freezing weather and frost? What would they do for insects? They eat only insects! And what about the humming birds that feed on blossoms on our farm and in our yard? We keep flowers growing for them. They like the nectar from these blossoms.

Horsemint is one of these.

Now where do the humming birds go? They are here to the end of the season. Suddenly they are gone! What voice speaks to tell them to go? This is very simple. The freeze and frost speak to them. They tell the humming birds it is time for them to go! Food will be scarce! There will be no more nectar from the flower blossoms for there will be no more blossoms. And "food" to any form of wildlife and to our own human species is something that speaks to all of us. Without food and water any species of life will soon perish.

Virginia Flycatchers and peewees leave when cold weather destroys the insects and flies! Yes, when cold weather slows the mosquitos, these wonderful birds fly South for winter! They go where there is food for them! And when spring returns to the North Temperate Zone they return to their old accepted places! But it is food that makes the humming bird, peewee, and Virginia flycatcher practical conscientious acceptors.

To me it is wonderful to live here in W-Hollow in Greenup County, Kentucky and to have all these bird, animal, reptilian, and lizard conscientious acceptors for my friends—and to know their ways of life, something about their ancestry and the histories of their survivals—in this North Temperate Zone. To know these now, and their survivals from prehistoric dates in their beginnings and survivals, makes me wonder about the survival of my human species. Will there be changes in us as we go into the future as there have been from the pre-dawn history of the lives of our little friends to our present day living in our back yard? I wonder about this.

MANIFEST DESTINY

Sitting at the kitchen table eating lunch with my wife, Naomi, and with Nola Claxton on this very, very bright winter day—bright with a canopy of blue above and white clouds floating and wind-driven! Suddenly, we heard a noise like the whirring of wings. Our kitchen, despite its six windows and the bright noontime daylight around us became dark enough to switch on the lights.

"What's happening?" Nola Claxton asked.

"Must be the autogiro following the pipeline," Naomi said.

"It's passed over here before and we heard its noisy engine," I said. "But it never darkened this kitchen. I'm going to see what is going on!"

I jumped up from my place at the end of the table which was the closest to the kitchen door and Naomi and Nola followed me outside. And we got out in time to see a flock of blackbirds that must have been gathered from West Virginia, Ohio, and Kentucky. They must have been getting together for weeks.

I would hate to try to estimate the number of birds in this flock that was still passing over. It would be as hard to estimate the dead leaves flying from the trees in a windy October storm. I had stood on earth and looked up into one of these storms where I thought I saw millions of leaves coming together, going apart—touching—swirling—laughing—having a wild autumn dance—to the wild strains of an autumn wind symphony.

But these birds were not buoyed upward, lifted and swirled, by the wild autumn winds like the air-light autumn leaves had been. Today these winds were strong, blowing over the valleys and hills—breaking branches from the leafless oaks. These winds were doing a great pruning job of eliminating dead branches and twigs from the tops of green trees—blowing down the dead trees still standing. It was a beautiful devastating wind—filled with wild music—a current of moving mass going on in the same direction that these millions of birds were going—birds that almost touched each other, talked to one another in flight; birds that darkened the sky, kept the sun's rays from the ground where dark shadows lay on earth's surface like rugs upon a floor.

I didn't speak. I would talk after the train of birds had gone over. I was so lifted up by this phenomemon in nature I doubt that I could have spoken at the moment. I'd never seen this many birds in one flock at anytime in my life and I'd seen some big flocks. This flock had to be two miles in length. It was about one-eighth mile wide.

Flying at full speed with the massive wind movement all over the wooded slope where Shinglemill Hollow junctions with W-Hollow—birds, tired of flight dropped down onto branches of the trees for a brief rest—and in a few seconds flew up into the mainstream of fluttering wings. They rejoined their companions. They knew where they were going. This was a movement—manifest destiny for these birds.

Nola and Naomi had stood quietly and in awe of this spectacle in nature. Our house had been in the direct path of these migratory birds. Food remained on our plates. Food on our plates and in the dishes would be getting cold. But excitement—a great spectacle in nature such as we were seeing could quench thirst and satisfy an appetite.

Even though the birds were rushing they had a beautiful day—temperature from middle to high thirties. White clouds were floating across an arch of azure blue. In the past week much rain had fallen—rain that had washed the atmosphere clean of any smog or Indian Summer haze particles of dust, particles of dead hanging white oak leaves, sycamore fuzzy, and blight from beeches. This was why this day was clean and bright—with white clouds, blue-azure skies—and with bright folds of laundried wind—dried and laundried by the sun, very weak at this season of the year—late November—almost the beginning of December.

Now, the tired birds were bringing up the rear. So many birds were alighting on poplar, oak, ash, maple, sourwood branches on the slope for Shinglemill Hollow and resting only for a few seconds, then rejoining the flight, in the mass-movement of the dancing, frolicking, jesturing—wild winds—a wild symphony that could be revised and recorded into the greatest earth music.

Now with the great flock of birds gone and the sun's getting down to remove the carpet-shadows from late autumn floor of earth—Naomi, Nola and I stood in our backyard, forgetting to return to the kitchen and finish our lunch.

"I never saw that many birds at one time in my life," said Nola Claxton. "Wonder where they were going."

"South—but South—deep South is a long way," Naomi said. "Jesse what are you thinking about?"

"Naomi, I wonder if flocks of birds have a memorized route they take," I said. "All flocks of migratory birds have come over this same route. Never has there been a flock to equal this one in the number of birds and the length of this bird train in flight. In the thirty-two years we've lived here, flocks of birds each autumn go over in this same direction! Naomi, you and I have watched them."

Birds in flight, robins, martins, blackbirds, peewees and Virginia Flycatchers, never accepted other birds—other than their own kind into their flocks when they gathered to migrate. They chose their own kind. Why was it this way? What was their bird instinct of grouping together and the preservation of their own specie of the bird family?

Yes, I was in silence but I was thinking about bird flights. Did birds select their leader or leaders? Or, did more positive and determined birds of the flock fly up to the front and take over the responsibilities of gathering up their kind and getting them into the skies for a long flight South or deep South? And did they have certain areas marked out along their migratory path for roosting? How did they manage flying high in the skies to get food? It took energy to propel their little wings on hundreds of miles of flight through cool winds, hostile currents of air—through rains, above frost, and over often a hostile countryside. Many areas over which they had to pass could be hostile to birds—and, more, especially to blackbirds, noted destructionists in farmers' fields of corn in August when corn begins to mature. Blackbirds could gather and destroy a field of corn, as they have mine in the Ohio River Valley bottoms—pecking through the green husk on the ear and stripping part of the soft green grains from the cob—what is left on the cob, sours—deteriorates—turns black, shrinks, decays. Farmers often shoot into these flocks of black birds destroying their corn.

Now in their flight South they have food. Do the leaders of the flocks know where cornfields are along their memorized path of flight—or, do they suddenly find one from the air and all swarm down onto it for a sumptious meal and rest after hours in flight? Here, gorge on corn quickly and get into the air again before the farmer comes with his gun?

Slowly, Naomi, Nola and I walked back into the kitchen and took our places at the table. Our food had grown cold now. And I was still thinking of the great flock of birds that I had just witnessed on their migratory path toward the South—birds riding and flying with the wind. How many would die on this journey?

But there had been great exoduses of people. Moses led his people, the Jews, from Egypt where they had been enslaved. They went back to their homeland, their promised land. This was a long hard journey to the "Promised Land."

Perhaps one of the most daring, dangerous mass exodus of people were those of different religious faiths living in one big country, India. India was partioned into West Pakistan and East Pakistan for the Moslems—and those of Hindu faith fled the Pakistans for India. It is estimated over a million people, Pakistan and Hindu, were murdered in these exoduses within a country of people trying to find safe homelands and freedom.

Then there were the great and continuous wagon trains taking our eastern Americans across a broad and dangerous west to settle in California. And there have been leaders, plans made, supplies taken for the long hard movement of families, men, women and children and their possessions from one country to another and a part of one country to another part. Plans have to be made and followed.

One of the greatest marches in the world was made by the Greek mercenary army who had gone to fight for Cyrus against Artaxerxes in 401 B.C. Cyrus was murdered and all the Greek generals had been tricked and killed. A trained Athenian, not militarily trained for the army, was made leader of trained Spartan soldiers, Xenophon, the Athenian was elected to take charge of the army which was without supplies and had to live from the country as they marched. Xenophon was two years' leading them back to their homeland. But he did and recorded this march in his journal, *Anabasis*, which is, I'll say, one of the ten greatest books in the world today.

Now, if the birds, especially those that we have just watched going in a full fast flight like a blockened quivering wind over a late autumn's silhouettes of leafless iron-tracery—if only their leaders had an alphabet and language—surely they have a speakable language they understand each other—but a written language they'd have memorable stories to tell about their migratory flights of hundreds of miles and their returning in the spring. They could write about who made the plans and directed the flights—their plans for sleeping in the trees—their plans for food for this they couldn't carry with them.

Sitting at the table we didn't continue eating cold foods. Maybe, we didn't know why we had come in and sat down at our places again. What we had seen had shaken us. We weren't doing any talking either. I was thinking about the movement of people and birds in great exoduses and migratory movements. People's great exoduses had been caused by human force—seldom for seeking a better homeland. Birds migrating were natural and seasonal extravagancies more colorful than the autumn seasons.

SNOWSTORM: A DOWNFALL OF BEAUTIFUL PHYSICAL POETRY

No wonder there was such exodus of blackbirds, more than two miles in length, eighth of a mile wide, enough to darken the sun and put shadows on our yard! No wonder there was such rush in their flight over their old migratory route—their manifest destiny to the South. They knew what was coming! I wish birds had written languages (I think each species has a spoken language) and one who predicts the weather would write a bird book and tell us humans how they predict it so accurately and so long in advance! No wonder those birds were leaving here yesterday. This snowstorm which began at daylight this morning will never overtake them. At the rate they were flying, they're too far South. I am watching a snowstorm the multi-million blackbird flock that passed over here yesterday couldn't fly through this morning.

I have seen here in late autumn and winter seasons, past and present, some of the most beautiful snowstorms I have ever seen. It seems here the late autumn-winter temperatures, low to middle thirties, are just right for snow. Not in Norway, Sweden, Finland, Northern Greece or Korea have I ever seen as beautiful snow fall as I am watching through the triple windows facing the W-Hollow road of my workroom-library built on top of our garage. Here is the best lookout into the W-Hollow Valley of any room in this house which spreads from bluff to bluff across Shinglemill Hollow—even over the Shinglemill Stream which flows through large tiles under our house—at about where the new living room and our bedroom join.

There is not any wind out there driving the snow. There is not even the slightest movement of the tops of tall trees over on Breadloaf Hill—which is now beginning to look like a huge loaf of bread with white icing spread over it. This snow is coming down with fluffy downy flakes—so close to each other there might be a flake to each square inch.

Out there beyond my room windows is a world of white. Even Breadloaf Hill is becoming obscure now. I can see the dim outline of the white backbone of the hill and the white trees for the snow is clinging to the barren bodies of the oaks—rough-barked bodies, branches, arm and finger twigs. So wonderful to see these white trees, that only yesterday looked like iron tracery etched against an arch of soft blue-azure sky. Now completely dressed in white—standing like tall ghosts, returned to earth for some purpose and very much saddened by what they had seen. Tall trees clothed in soft white snow that cling tenaciously to all parts of their bodies from the large rough-barked trunks and bodies to their fingertipped twigs.

How in the world, I wondered as I looked out at this white beautiful world, could multi-millions of birds ever fly through the thickness of this falling snow? How could they look about and find their migratory path they followed going South? And what about food supplies now? Snow had covered the earth. This was not the day for bird flying. That day was when birds rode on the fast currents of wind blowing in the direction of their flight. This wind gave extra mileage in faster pursuit of their manifest destiny—which was somewhere in the South or deep South where they would find a new warm home for the winter months ahead. Come spring they would return to their homeland, which was in this Tri-State Area—and there being so many birds I felt sure they gathered for this flight from West Virginia, Ohio and Kentucky.

Now, I sat making notes on what I would write later about this snow. Seeing a storm such as this one, I didn't want to sit writing about it while I looked through my three windows with curtains tied back. And I wasn't going to write about it now. I wanted to sit back, enjoy it to the fullest! There is something beautiful about the great movements in nature—about the flora and fauna on the earth's surface in all its seasons—something great in the colors from white snow to red sunsets. And some great music—lyrics and symphonies in the winds and great extravaganzas such as we had yesterday all over these valleys and hills. All of these great movements of birds, autumn leaves carried by winds, water rushing in torrents down the streams—all of these are physical poems. This snowstorm before me is a beautiful poem.

Snow falling fluffy and furious, zigzagging down to the earth's floor without the help of wind has a preening sound. Stand out in it, as I will after while, look up at the grey-depths about—let the soft flakes hit your face and fall into your opened eyes. What a sensation! Then listen for the preening sound—that sweet little sound barely audible to the best of human ears! But that sound is there! Now, I'm sitting and watching a late-autumn physical poem. But I would rather be involved in that physical poem as to be watching its beauty through window glass. I'd rather feel, taste—love—be among and fondle the snowflakes as to be sitting here watching the poetry out there!

The white straight downward flow of snow! Snow, snow, like winter rain—downward, downward to the ground—there a white blanket to cover the winter scarred face of the earth! Snow, snow, snow! Not any November wind to blow. All winds right now are asleep. Poetry out there! Poetry out there! Beautiful poetry! Poetry out there as sure as positive as there is an eternity!

What a poem I am watching! Yesterday it was the body and the flow of massive wind—an unseen body but it was there and I always think I can see the wind—that solid body of slightly-silvered flowering stuff when the sun is shining. And today, it is snow! I never dreamed this would be happening today when I went to bed last night. How could we have a day like yesterday and a day to follow like today! What a great change in twenty-four hours. Two entirely different physical poems in twenty-four hours! How interesting it is to live within one mile of where I was born in W-Hollow, a North Temperate Zone where we have four distinct seasons of the year!

Relaxed to the beauty of reaching a high point of enjoyment such as I have reached when I have played Beethoven's Sixth Symphony—and when I play this I know he's the greatest composer who has ever lived—and to play this makes me wish I'd have been a composer—and starved more than being a writer—and copied some of the wind symphonies and wild wind extravaganzas I've heard—just copied them when sitting out and listening and then revised later; just been as wild about writing earth music as I've been about writing books—I've done books in one day, seven days, eight days, three weeks. I've written madly and wildly and I think as a composer, I could have produced—classical type—not anything cheap.

Maybe a winter symphony—one without the wild sounds of wind—but one with the soft sounds of preening snow—something when all the winter trees are white snow-covered ghosts and look very sad.

I came up to my workrrom above the garage at seven. At six-thirty, I'd sat at our breakfast table and listened to WLW, Cincinnati radio news. We do this each morning—where we heard there was a six inch snow in that area and all schools were closed and the snow was coming our way—up the Ohio River—and when this announcement was made I clapped my hands at the breakfast table and said: "Thank God for beautiful snow."

Maybe Naomi who sat across the table from me was less enthusiastic. At our breakfast table we could see the beautiful flakes "peppering down" and I got up from the table and turned on the lights out to the room in our back yard where I used to work. With these lights on along our back yard walk we could see the snowflakes falling. They were really "peppering down" and had covered our back yard walk and yard before we finished breakfast. The snowstorm coming up the Ohio River from Cincinnati had really reached us.

This is why just as soon as I had finished my breakfast, I went upstairs and turned on the light in my workroom. It was here I looked out very early into dim W-Hollow—with the downfall of beautiful physical poetry. It is here I am still at ten o'clock watching the downpour which has covered the meadows, the hillslopes and all the trees. It is really a white world here now. For three hours I've sat in ecstasy. I've watched the beauty of a snow-white physical poem. Thoughts have raced through my mind. I've taken notes which I will expand later and put on paper.

Right now I shall leave this room to get involved in the physical snow poem I've been watching. What a great three hours I've had. I expect to have another hour of physical enjoyment. I am now leaving this room—and I walk downstairs and get a wool sweater from the old living room press. Now I feel I'm sufficiently dressed to walk out into this snowstorm and be a part of this. Standing amid the down-coming fluffy flakes, one to each square inch, I lift my face toward the Heavens. The flakes hit my face. They fall into my opened eyes. Since I am hatless, hair on my head is white with snow.

This is it. I am a part. I am a part of this great physical poem. I am involved—and the sensation and ecstasy of being a part of this is great! I know it is great! This is a sensation! It's a great sensation. I'm filled with ecstasy. And when I'm chilled enough to leave this snow, I'll go back to my upstairs library and workroom over our garage and try to record what I have seen and describe how emotional I have been to rejoice in this beautiful and great day in nature that I have lived and loved.

W-Hollow Road in the snow

Photo by G. Sam Piatt

THE SUN'S UNDOING

Can I believe after yesterday the great snowstorm and the day before the great exodus of birds that we would have a third day following the other two like this? Well, we have another different but beautiful day. We have an opposite beauty to the other two but it has been a fantastic, beautiful day.

This morning at six and an hour before daybreak, I looked at our backdoor thermometer and it was twenty degrees above. Naomi had switched the back yard lights on and we could observe a minute portion of our world—a microscopic bit of the wonderland we could expect at daybreak.

The ground was so frozen that it was heaved up in certain spots—and each blade of grass was a stiff white spear. It was stiff with frost and perhaps, with a thin coating of ice. Weather reports last night said the snow would turn to rain and melt the snow—and the night would turn colder—and there would be a freeze. The weather change must have been so abrupt that rain on the bodies and branches of trees froze before it could run down the rough bark off to the ground.

The lights in our back yard shining on the holly trees, lilac bushes, the dogwoods, walnuts and poplar trees, made their bodies glisten. They sparkled like decorated Christmas trees. I could hardly wait for daylight to see our third new world in three days. What change! What variety!

From my place at the end of the table I could look out into our back yard at the trees glistening in the light! First, I had a large tumbler of juice, then small hot biscuits and an egg that had been fried in a skillet where our steaks last night had been grilled. Then I had honey-clear sorghum molasses to pour over hot biscuits—and I had good coffee, made from our well-water to drink as hot as I could stand with my good breakfast. I had this good breakfast and a new exciting world I would be viewing from the windows of my workroom and library over our garage. And I could be out in the world too—touching the frozen twigs, breathing the air—feeling the stiff spears of frosted frozen grass with my shoe leather. I would be viewing our valley—the contours of tree-white glistening slopes! This would come in a matter of minutes! Right now I was eating a stout breakfast and enjoying my coffee.

"We're having one exciting day after another," Naomi said. "I'll never forget that long black cloud of birds that went over here and shut out the sun. Nor will I ever forget the beauty of yesterday's snow! Today is going to be another one of a different beauty."

From where we lived we had to drive twenty-five miles to see a movie! We wouldn't meet people who were interested in writing and the arts. They weren't around! And where could we go to hear a good symphony or to see a good play? I didn't know where—perhaps, not in a hundred-mile radius.

There is a saying when one doesn't have high-level things to go see and hear then he finds his high-level substitutes. Nature was now furnishing them without cost. What people who were seeking the man-made creative things would have given to have seen and heard what we had seen and heard in the last two days and would be seeing today.

After breakfast a slow daylight was coming to the W-Hollow Valley. All indicative signs pointed to much fog-like white clouds sitting down on the meadows in many places. Now, I left the table, walked up into my workroom library over our garage—best room in this house in which to work or to view the W-Hollow Valley. Despite the patches of lazy fog, rolled up like huge bales of cotton and resting on our meadows down the valley, I could see a meadow floor where day before yesterday the grass was green and from eight inches to a foot tall. Now that grass was a white floor, each blade a white frozen stiff spear of frost and ice.

The telephone and electric wires were weighted white wires—weighted with ice and frost and swaying between the poles over which electricity and voices came. Even there was ice frozen over water in puddle holes along our narrow one-car lane road. And there were filigrees of frost seemingly on each gravel—each clump of grass that bordered our lane road. Our rail fence this morning was made with white rails. It was a ghost rail fence.

There was not any sun rising. There was not even a light place in the sky where the morning sun ought to be. The world was misty dark, a semi-light world—"When would the sun be breaking through?" I thought. "Never, never," flashed through my mind. "Let our W-Hollow world stay like this for awhile. We need this kind of world. We need this world of winter beauty for the old and the young—especially the young. This will make poets of a few of our youth! This is physical poetry! Today is another great and beautiful poem!"

On Breadloaf Hill the tall and short trees were brilliantly white and glistening in the morning lights. Each tree looked like it had been decorated for Christmas pageantry. But human decorators couldn't have done the job as artistically as Nature had done it last night. The rain wetting snow and then clear skies, the drop in temperature and the frost that was equal to a mild snow had done this. The trees on Breadloaf Hill yesterday were white and soft with snow. They looked like disconsolate ghosts that had come back to earth and had been saddened by what they had seen. Yesterday: Snow poem, beautiful. Today: ice-and-frost poem, more beautiful! Here I sat in an awe of ecstasy looking at the W-Hollow Valley, the lane road, rail fence and the trees on Breadloaf Hill.

The trees in our yard were in a sheer white

brilliance. Grass all over our yard—little white spears of brilliance. And here was our home in the center of this W-Hollow world. This beautiful world—our world—one we're glad to be living in and to be a part of—our world, filled with beauty and excitement—one day after another on and on—our world for three days great physical poems and great natural symphonies.

How long could I sit by this window looking out into the beauties of this great physical poem! Same as when we had the snow I would have to get out, to touch, to feel, to be with—to feel my shoe leather on the spears of the frosted grass. I would have to breathe the good cool air and feel the chill of wind and walk and walk and walk and feel-and-see, feel-and-see, and feel-and-see!

When I walked onto the porch bareheaded but wearing a wool jacket, I had a warm comfortable feeling over my body. But to breathe this fresh uncontaminated air was like drinking cold pure spring water. I looked at the thermometer. It was twenty-two above. Now I walked onto the frozen blades of grass—ice and frost covered—some straight and some curled. They lay matted on either side of our front walk like a white carpet—an extraordinary one, but not expensive. Nature had made this decoration to cover the scarred floor of the earth.

Now when I first stepped from the porch and put my leather shoe sole onto this frozen decorative carpet—with two-hundred ten pounds of weight bearing down on the leather—there was a crunch sound. And I could feel this crunch through my shoe leather into my feet, up my legs and into my body. This was a pleasant feeling, a little sensation which I never obtained when walking on some of the finest carpets in the finest homes and hotels of America—and in foreign lands, Europe and Iran, the Pakistans and India. I couldn't remember when I had breathed air as clean and cool as this W-Hollow air this morning. I couldn't taste this air in my nostrils but I could feel the coolness with each inhale and exhale to enter and leave my lungs.

I walked over the beautiful decorative carpet where heavy yard grass grew in spring, summer and up until middle autumn and even after first frosts. I left behind my tracks, little indentations that pressed down the frozen-fluff that was so brilliant in the morning light. I walked down into our lane road—where there were puddle holes ice-covered—sometimes a thin carpet shining in the morning air and sometimes not any carpet. To my surprise, after all the rain and snow that had fallen I could kick up the dust on our lane road.

Then, above there was visibility. Still, the sun hadn't broken through. There was a dim white ball above a darkness—a thin sky roof—and, there were clouds of fog that had been sitting on the creek meadows resting—lifting up—ascending slowly. In over a half century, I'd not seen anything in this like I was seeing this morning. I'd not seen anything like the snow I'd seen yesterday and the biggest exodus of birds I'd seen the day before yesterday.

At ten fifty-two a.m. it happened. The sun

broke through while I was looking up watching the white ball beyond the murky thin ravished disturbed patch of sky roof. I looked suddenly at my watch to get the time of day. The sun's breaking through changed the whole valley. Ice and frost that clothed the bodies, branches, arms and finger twigs of all the trees—even the rock cliffs—rail fence—and partly frozen-over W-Hollow stream.

Now, I was for once standing in the most magnificent fairy land, a make-believe world—only the most imaginative of imaginations could conjure up a world like this. If a man driving across W-Hollow could see this, if he didn't stop his car and get out to see this—to stand in awe of Nature's magnificence—I'd be surprised. He wouldn't be man who had rational intelligence above all other living things on wings, legs, fins, and that crawled upon this earth.

Here was the polished silvered white forests, white streams, white rail and board fences—all glistening in the late November sun. And now was my time to photograph them forever in my mind. I could get a mental picture of this great physical poem as I'd remember the ones I memorized yesterday and the day before. This would never come again. And, the sun as weak as it was—great beauty and symbol in Nature, would in less than an hour erase all this beauty from the W-Hollow earth. It had begun to do this now. There were streams of mists going up from the shining trees, mists rising toward the sun from all this beautiful white earth. The sun was undoing the most beautiful world I'd ever seen. Frost is a beautiful substance that in the sunlight can sparkle like diamonds and in less than a minute change from sparkling frost-diamonds to cloud mists and be ascending upwards in small white clouds. This is what was happening now.

Naomi came onto the porch dressed to go to Greenup. She closed the door and held the car keys in her hand.

"What a beautiful day," she said. "I've never seen W-Hollow prettier than at this minute."

"But it won't last long," I said. "The sun broke through the clouds less than an hour ago. Now its melting the frost and ice. And this is changing our white glistening diamond world. Our fairyland dream-world like this will never come again!"

"You want to go to Greenup with me?" she asked.

"Yes, I do," I replied quickly. "I want to see this world along Womack Hollow on the W-Hollow Road." From our house to there was a fraction more than a half mile. When we went over The Gap—the divide between W-Hollow and Womack Hollow, we changed worlds again. And this was hard to believe in such short distance.

Womack Hollow was the same as W-Hollow had been early in the morning. It was a white glistening diamond world. There was not any mists going up from the trees. The sun hadn't broken through these murky skies.

"Have you ever seen such change?" I asked Naomi.

"No, W-Hollow filled with sunlight and clouds ascending. And the woods losing their sparkling white clothing and turning dark again!"

The W-Hollow Road going down Womack Hollow with barren flora and fauna, on either side but leafless now—but a white-ghost forest, a sparkling forest. Our driving down this road was like going through a white sparkling tunnel. There was a sparkling tunnel roof of trees interlacing branches overhead.

When we reached the Sandy River Road, there was a roof of fog about the Sandy River that spread from hilltop to hilltop on either side thus roofing in the Valley and keeping out the sun. What a beautiful drive this was now. Nature had painted everything along this State Highway. Even tin cans in the ditches, for the first time, became beautiful.

"Don't you like to ride along this highway now," Naomi asked me.

"I wish it could be this way all the time," I said. "No, I change my mind. Too much of the same can become disgusting. I'd chose variety. I'd say: 'Nature you do it! You make the changes!' And I think Nature can give us great variety."

Now, we had come to the end of State Route One. Here it junctioned with U.S. Twenty-three. And here in this broad Ohio River Valley there was fog overcast—a roof across the five mile wide valley. A frost and ice covered sparkling world and not any sun!

"We've just found sun in W-Hollow," Naomi said.

And we had just found sun in W-Hollow and by now all the frost and thin ice had changed due to bright sunball's undoing!

Our W-Hollow world had returned to its late autumn's natural colors. What an exciting world was our small world in which we were living now!

WINDS

I walk into the W-Hollow wind in my valley! This is a February wind. The temperature this morning was twenty-four but now it is forty-eight. It is afternoon. The sun is shining. The sky is blue. And this wind is blowing—perhaps—twenty-five miles an hour.

Now, with this wind around me—this fresh fluid substance that howls up this valley and bends the dark barren boughs on the oaks—breaks twigs and rustles among the brown tough-butted white oak leaves still clinging to the boughs!

How good it is to feel this wind against my face! How hard it presses against my body—with my over two-hundred pounds I stand firm. I stand like a tree that is planted by a wet weather spring in a deep little fertile valley, until I get ready to walk. Then, I walk, going the same way this wind is blowing. It pushes me along until I decide to stop here. I brace my feet and stop.

Upon the hill above me is a patch of brown broomsedge that bends when the winds blow. This brown broomsedge lies low—until the wind passes over and is gone. Then it rises up to stand until another avalanche comes along—an avalanche of unseen wind, strong and mighty—and bows again.

Here I stand and breathe deeply and let the

wind blow. The wind is reciting poetry to me. It is talking to me. It is playing music! How wonderful to stand and listen to the wind and to turn away from the senseless chatter of man! How good it is to feel this soft substance swirling all around me and over me and to breathe of it. How wonderful to be alive and up in the wind instead of not being able to breathe this wind and lying shoulder deep in the rind of earth without space or light—shut off eternally from the bright wind, all its words, music, and poetry.

I heard once the October winds blow over the plains in Old Persia, which is now Iran. It is an old land where Medes and Persians lived and fought. These were troubled winds when they blew near the ruins of the old Persepolis, once capitol of Old Persia—a city that once was powerful but is no more. Winds sang lonesome here and among the yellow leaves on the aspen trees. Winds sang loud and lonesome over the land the Persians used to irrigate and farm. But this was partially dry and arid now. This land, once a Persian breadbasket, wasn't farmed. It was a barren land over which the Persian winds sang for what had been! Whose Persian hands had fondled this dirt and how many centuries ago?

Not too far distant from Persepolis, I heard winds singing in the pines—and there were the old fire temples in a world where Goodness had once been light and Evil had been darkness.

I heard more winds singing up in this high country than in any semi-arid land away from the sound of the sea! I heard winds singing in

Teheran, Esfahan, Shiraz, and Meshed. What a world of wind sounds I heard in the world of old Persia traveling over much of it by car! Standing on the plains where the Medes and Persians marched and fought, I heard winds crying and grieving for a life that had been but was no more.

In my W-Hollow I've heard the day and night winds crying and sighing in spring, summer, autumn, and winter. I have heard the soft spring winds blowing among the tender green leaves as I have walked under my woods at night. I have stood and listened to the tender voices of spring winds.

I have heard wild summer winds blowing harshly before a summer storm! I have heard the summer winds talking to the blades of growing corn. I have heard them combing the ripening wheat—the golden wheat—summer winds hunting and searching for something. I have heard them in the poplar leaves—the large slick-bellied poplar leaves where winds and leaves spoke big words to each other.

In autumn I have gone to the woods at night to hear the winds in the dying leaves. I have gone to hear winds sweep the leaves from the trees and blow them like flocks of birds to hit my face! I've stood among these leaves the winds carried against me, around me, over me! I have heard the music in the wind among the dead leaves on trees on my W-Hollow hills in the night. And this music was good to hear.

In the autumn days I saw the leaves like flocks of multi-colored birds carried by the singing autumn winds over the old fields, hill slopes, and into the valleys. This was autumn wind music such as I never heard in any other country, I heard it here until I said I'd never spend another autumn in any country where there were no multi-colored leaves! I wanted to hear the winds among these leaves. I wanted to see leaves flying hither and thither in the bright autumn air over the hills and the valleys I call home!

Now I hear a sadness in my February winds blowing among the leafless oak branches and soughing among the needles on the fingers, hands, and arms of pines on these W-Hollow slopes. I heard this among pines in the grove behind our house! I have felt a chill in the winds and I have heard a winter sadness not akin to somber music.

Here the afternoon February winds are crying! And the iron tracery of these mighty oaks swish at the blowing winds—slicing them—slicing their bodies into the unseen and shapeless slices that join again with their bodies of winds from which they were sliced. Sometimes they don't slice but blow in different directions. They change courses. Here I wish I could read the poetry the winds are saying! I wish I could interpret the whispers I believe I hear! What a night this is! It is colorful time out in a space of the world.

But talk about a land where the winds are always blowing! This is the home of my father's ancestors. This is Scotland where I lived for a year—and where I climbed the mountain slopes where grew the heather and the whin—or the broom! There was scarcely a place in Scotland where I could not hear the wind blow or hear the sound of water. The sound of wind on a long, dark winter night in Scotland is something unforgettable. It is something to walk over a Scottish moor in winter and face the wind and hunt for a white hare in the snow! As a younger man I used to wonder why the winter winds cried so plaintively over the Scottish moors and among the heather and the whin—and among the bracken on the slopes! I used to wonder if they cried for Scottish clansmen that fell in battle—including my ancestors there—winds crying in Scotland for what has been and is no more in that mountainous rugged land, the home of my father's ancestors—a land from whence my name came. Sounds of night winds blowing over, night winds crying so well yet unremembered through the years!

There are no more winter-sad winds blowing in W-Hollow, in Kentucky, and in Scotland than there are in Greece where everyplace and in all the seasons I heard the sadness in the blowing winds and in the sounds of water.

Take a night in Greece—take a night in Corinth—and hear the winds blowing among the cypress trees. In Greece the cypress is symbolic of death. The cypress often marks the graves of their ancient dead. And the cypresses often grow over the ruins where a city has been—such as Old Corinth.

In Corinth I have stood and listened to the

night winds blowing—swishing sadly through the cypress tops above the ancient dead and above the ruins of Old Corinth still not excavated. I have heard the winds blow over the Theban Plains, cry among the cypresses and olive orchards of Delphi, and sing over Parnassus, the sacred mountain for poets! I have heard the sacred winds come in from the Aegean Sea to blow over Attica—from her southern most land tip at Sunion up over this hallowed land—among the branches of the ancient olives to Athens. These were the winds that Socrates, Plato, Xenophon, and Aristotle walked the streets of Athens to hear! Athenian winds I have heard around 'the rock' on many a night, and I wished for them to blow sounds back to me—the voices of Socrates, Plato, and Aristotle—just to hear their voices on the wind one time.

Egypt has joyful and friendly winds. Naomi, our daughter Jane, and I lived on the bank of the mighty Nile for one year. We lived there long enough to know Egypt has benevolent winds. The Pharaohs knew this in their colorful days of rich living in antiquity. They rode in splendor and style on the Nile, waving to their subjects who lived on the Nile River banks. They rode on rose-decked feluccas, with a sail and the ever-blowing, one-way winds that pushed them gaily up the Nile, up-current to their destination. And after reaching their destination they lowered the sail and the swift current in the Nile brought them downstream. How many times we rode up-Nile with the benevolent Egyptian winds at our backs and later lowered the sail and let the Nile current bring our felucca back to Gezira Island and home!

In this land where Ra Atem, the Sun, was once a god, his subjects lived on the east bank of the Nile where the sun arose and this meant life; but when they died they were buried on the west bank of the Nile, which was in the direction of sunset and this meant death.

Here in this ancient land Cleopatra, Egypt's most beautiful Queen—riding in queenly attire, with members of her court and her subjects around her—felt, knew, and loved these benevolent winds of Egypt blowing freight cargoes and pleasure boats up the Nile.

Naomi, Jane, and I spent time on our balcony feeling and breathing the fresh wind blowing up the Nile. This wind blew cool at night until we had to sleep under blankets. Winds and sunlight were everywhere in Egypt. There were the eternal Nile winds and the Hamsoon winds that blew in their season over the Sahara and lifted clouds of sand into the air that made Egypt a murky land for days. But Egypt is the home of unforgettable winds.

Now, I walk in this world where I was born and grew to manhood loving the winds in all the seasons! So often I have wished I had learned music. Had I learned music so I could have been a composer, I feel that I could have captured these sounds into a great symphony, this music of the winds I have heard! I walk in the wind. I breathe deeply of the wind. I feel it hit my face. I feel the blowing wind hit my face as I walk slowly back toward my home. My house has walls that separate me from the wind. But I love this wind. It is music. This wind is poetry. It talks and whispers to me and I talk and whisper to it. These winds and I are one.

Jesse Stuart's walk at W-Hollow where the blue larkspur bloom

THE COLOR OF THE STORM

The sultry summer day yesterday brought shimmering heat, last night, and eventually, thunder and lightning. This morning the sky was overcast and we thought a storm was approaching. I sat on the front porch and observed the great green clouds of leaves. My father and Uncle Jesse Hilton always told me when the leaves spiraled up toward the sky to expect rain.

Now the oak leaves were twisting up from the strong, sturdy, boughs. The oak leaves had turned over, showing their soapy bellies to the wind and hot sun. If one observed closely he knew Nature was getting out of time, and something was about to happen. Now, soft winds began blowing and the green soft leaves rattled as if their throats were dry and they were asking for water.

The winds came faster and I knew there was something behind all of this. I got up from my chair on the porch and walked down the walk. I looked North toward Ohio, the way rains come, and there I saw, very low, on the horizon, just over the treetops, long, thin, racing clouds. Their bellies were as thin as those of fast-racing greyhounds! Behind these clouds was a smooth, gray cloud. This was it! This was the storm cloud. This one would bring the rain.

I never knew a storm had color until now. The leaves, pressed by the forerunners of messenger winds, were not a soft green as usual. But they had a pale, dry appearance. Many leaves with lighter undersides, such as the poplar, turned their lighter shades toward the wind and approaching storm. Even the leaves were different. My father and Uncle Jesse had been right about the leaves and the storm.

Then, I looked down the valley toward Moore's Hill. I saw something I had seen before, but never as effective, and as beautiful! The great winds were carrying loads of rain across the earth in waves as if they were using this water from the skies to mop the earth, and everything growing thereon. These waves of water, carried by the wind, one after the other, were as white as clouds. They came into view and passed out of sight, while the small and giant trees bowed to the breaking point for almost thirty minutes while this storm passed over.

THE HUMMINGBIRD IN THE GARDEN

Hummingbird, there is not now nor has there ever been, a bird like you! You are a combination of jet and helicopter . . . more than these two combined. You can rise from a flower and soar up through the windy skies toward a white cloud so fast it's hard to follow you with our natural eyesight. You are that fast moving forward, and you can fly backwards just as fast. A jet can't do that!

You stand in the air like a helicopter while you draw sweet nectar from the blue larkspur along our walk with a bill almost as long as your body. You fly from the bottom up to each blossom on the larkspur until you reach the top. Then you fly over to another larkspur . . . if you miss a blossom you back up to get it. I like to see you go into reverse and fly backwards.

Our engineers would like to know your secret. Maybe they can follow the designs that the Creative Engineer figured out when he designed you the size of a man's thumb, with a pressurized body to stand great speed and air currents, up toward the skies and down to earth. How our engineers would like to build a jet that can fly up and down, forward and backward at terrific speed, and one that can stand in the air like a helicopter!

Hummingbird, I marvel at your creation. In our world of birds, you stand alone, From the time I have been able to walk and to know what things were in the world about me, I have admired you. I used to wish that I could fly from flower to flower, gather my food like you, then take off faster than an approaching storm.

Hummingbird, your food from the flowers fascinates me. The sweets from wildwood flowers give you strength. It is such a little bit of sustenance that I wonder how it can give you your great speed and endurance.

I have watched you cover all the blue larkspur on the right side of my walk. Now you cross over to the left side. Each blossom you barely touch with your slender bill and then you move on to another.

Another wonderful thing is the way you get the gold dust of pollen on your bill. You carry it from male to female and pollinate the female and bring a better production of fruit, berries, grain and vegetables!

Maybe that is why the Great Creative Engineer made you . . . to help mankind, as well as provide something beautiful to see. He really worked on your design. He made you to use the special fuel that is sweet and beautiful because it comes from the most beautiful resources on earth, the flowers.

Hummingbird, I'd like to stand here and watch you fly to your nest. I wonder if you gathered nectar from my flowers this morning to take home to little hummingbirds. Perhaps your nest is high in the top of the tallest tree, out on a small swinging branch with large green leaves to protect it from the rain. You make the quick trips to the nest, no matter how far away, with a load of wild, sweet nectar.

Wonderful little streamliner with the greatest power of flight in the world, I wonder about you. I have always wanted to see the eggs in your nest, the little birds and to watch you feed them. I have wanted to follow you to your home and I have tried—but always have failed. I want to know more about you.

You are a spirit of beauty and you are poetry, too. You live up in an ethereal world except when you come down for food among the flowers.

I wonder where you are in the winter. Where do you go? Do you go South to that vacationland where flowers bloom and the sun is always warm? Do you know another country and its skies like you know this country and these skies? I wish you could tell me before you finish the blue larkspur on the other side of this walk.

You are sensible about the seasons. You don't come too early or too late. When we see the thousands of flower petals upon our warm spring earth and smell their fragrance on the winds of spring, we look around for you and you will be here.

And in the autumn, when September days are still warm, you buzz to the farewell-to-summer wild phlox along the streams, and to the sumac, daisy, ironweed, silkweed and queen of the meadow. I see you around here enjoying early autumn just as much as I.

You must observe the few sassafras leaves that have turned red and have fallen as you fly above a changing earth. A few sumac leaves have colored without the help of cold weather and have fallen. When you see these changes, you go away. We never know when you leave. But when you go, after we no longer see you on the flowers, in three days—often less time—we can expect frost.

Hummingbird, who tells you about these things? Your judgement is uncanny. How do you know? Somebody has to tell you. Where do you get the message and from whom? Do you hear a whisper in the wind?

Hummingbird, you live in the wind and you sleep at night high on a swinging bough where only a few birds can find you. If you fly at night it's toward the moon and stars. In the morning you fly and face the sun. In the evening you watch the sunset. Your long bill gets golddusty with pollen and you ride the winds and feel the storms. Your thoughts must be lofty ones. You are in heart and mind a poet. You cannot be anything else.

I wish you could tell me the flower you like best. I think I know which it is. It's the old fashioned horsemint. That is why I have planted it all over this yard. I want you to come and visit me often.

Acknowledgements

"I live in Three Houses," "Constructionists Versus Destructionists," "Conscientious Acceptors," and "Winds" first appeared in *The Tennessee Teacher* and are reprinted by permission of the Tennessee Education Association.

"The Colors Winter Wears", "Needed . . . A National Cleanup Day!", and "A New Garden of Eden?" were first published in *American Forest* and are reprinted by permission of the American Forestry Association.

"Manifest Destiny," "Snowstorm: A Downfall of Beautiful Physical Poetry," and "The Sun's Undoing" first appeared in *Scimitar and Song* and are reprinted with their permission.

"Lost Sandstones and Lonely Skies" first appeared in the *Southwest Review* and is reprinted by permission of the Southern Methodist University Press.

"In Moments of Reflection" was first published in *Educational Forum* and is reprinted by permission of Kappa Delta Pi, P. O. Box A, West Lafayette, IN 47906, owners of the copyright.

"The Hummingbird in the Garden" first appeared in *National Wildlife*, Copyright 1963 by the National Wildlife Federation. Reprinted with their permission from the June-July issue of *National Wildlife* magazine.

"When Heart and Death Lie Down Together in a Lonely Land" first appeared in the Sept. 1958 issue of *The American Book Collector.*

"Are We a Nation of Digits?" reprinted from *The Saturday Evening Post* © 1962 The Curtis Publishing Company.

"The People I Meet" first appeared in *English Journal* in March 1972.

"The Simple Joys" appeared in the *Country Beautiful Holiday Issue,* reprinted with permission.

"The Simple Joys of Snow" appeared originally in *The Angels.*

Great care has been taken to find the owners of copyrighted materials and to make due acknowledgement. We will gladly rectify any omissions in future editions.

The photographs used throughout this book are from the Jesse Stuart family album.